Bus & Recognition

4th Edition

ALAN MILLAR

IAN ALLAN
Publishing

FRONT COVER:
A Mercedes-Benz Vario O814D with Plaxton Beaver 2 minibus body operated by Arriva The Shires. **Plaxton**

BACK COVER, UPPER:
A Plaxton Pointer-bodied Dennis Dart SLF of Red Bus, the North Devon subsidiary of the Cawlett group which runs former National Bus Company routes in parts of southwest England. **Plaxton**

BACK COVER, LOWER:
Universitybus, a wholly-owned subsidiary of the University of Hertfordshire, operates several Dennis Dart SLFs with Wright Crusader bodies. This is the first with a Floline ramped floor. **Wright**

TITLE PAGE:
Plaxton Viewmaster: The highfloor Viewmaster coach, with deeper windscreen and standard Supreme side glasses, is seen here on a Volvo B10M in Birmingham (see page 129).

First published 1998

ISBN 0 7110 2598 3

© Ian Allan Publishing Ltd 1998

Published by Ian Allan Publishing

an imprint of Ian Allan Publishing Ltd, Terminal House, Station Approach, Shepperton, Surrey TW17 8AS.
Printed by Ian Allan Printing Ltd, Riverdene Business Park, Molesey Road, Hersham, Surrey KT12 4RG.

Code: 9808/C2

Picture Credits: All photographs are by the author unless credited otherwise.

LEFT: *Mercedes-Benz 811D: A Nottingham 811 minibus with one of the last Dormobile bodies built before that company, famous for 1950s and 1960s motor caravans it had long since ceased to make, went out of business (see page 142).*

2

Contents

Part 1.
DOUBLE-DECK BUSES

Part 2.
SINGLE-DECK BUSES

Part 3.
COACHES

Part 4.
MINIBUSES

CHASSIS AND BASE VANS

BODIES AND COMPLETE VEHICLES

BELOW: *Jonckheere: A Deauville P599 body on a Mercedes-Benz OH1628L chassis, a model only sold in Britain under a small batch of these bodies. It was part of a batch bought by Redwing of London for its Evan Evans Tours contracts, carrying tourists from London hotels on day trips from the capital.us (see page 119).*

Introduction

Welcome to the 4th edition of *abc Bus & Coach Recognition*.

If you are just beginning to become interested in buses and coaches, and want to know more about the vehicles you see on Britain's roads, then I hope that this book will help you identify and understand the differences and similarities between the various types. If your interest is longer established, I hope you will find that it provides a useful résumé of the buses and coaches in service today — and especially of the many types introduced since the 3rd edition was published six years ago.

Buses and coaches are expensive pieces of capital equipment which their owners expect to last a long time. The latest generation of lowfloor double-deckers, for example, cost around £140,000 each and it's not unknown for very high specification luxury coaches to cost double that. Most major operators expect their larger buses to last around 15 years before they sell some of them on to secondary operators for further service. And that is just the average. Despite heavy recent investment, some bus operators still run vehicles they bought around 20 years ago, and, in London, the exceptional case of the Routemaster means there are buses in regular weekday service which were built nearly 40 years ago.

Another way of looking at it is to say that many of today's buses and coaches were built by manufacturers and supplied to operators which have nearly all since disappeared.

In the 1970s, most bus operators were in public ownership. The state-owned National Bus Company and Scottish Bus Group between them ran around 25,000 buses and coaches in England, Wales and Scotland; London Transport, under local authority control, operated another 6,000; seven local authority-controlled Passenger Transport Executives (PTEs) ran 10,000 buses between them in the West Midlands, Merseyside, Greater Manchester, South Yorkshire, West Yorkshire, Tyne & Wear and Greater Glasgow; and another 50 local authorities ran over 6,000 vehicles. Demand for new buses was stimulated by a government grant scheme which, for most of the decade, met half of the cost of vehicles suitable for one-person operation.

Vehicle supply was dominated by British Leyland (BL), formed in 1968 and itself in state ownership from 1975. Although it gradually applied the Leyland name to products across its range, BL didn't immediately eliminate the AEC, Daimler and Bristol brands; it also owned the bodybuilders Park Royal, Charles Roe and ECW, and built complete vehicles at its Leyland National plant in Workington.

American-owned Bedford and Ford's lightweight coach and rural bus chassis were bought in large quantities by independent operators and some public sector fleets; imports, led most successfully by Volvo and Scania, began to establish a foothold. By the end of the decade, Dennis was also re-establishing itself in the market and MCW was a major force.

Huge upheaval in the 1980s deregulated coach and bus services and route tendering was introduced in London. Most public sector operators have been privatised since 1986 and, at the time of writing, the industry is dominated by the London stock exchange-listed Stagecoach, FirstGroup,

Arriva, National Express and Go Ahead groups which, between them, operate around 28,000 buses in Britain and more in Europe and other continents.

Other larger operators — MTL, Yorkshire Traction, London United (owned by French group Transdev), East Yorkshire, Wellglade, Metroline (London-based and stock exchange-listed), Blazefield, Cawlett and Southern Vectis — operate another 5,000 vehicles. There are nearly 3,000 more with the 17 surviving municipal fleets.

New bus grant was phased out by 1984, killing much of the demand for double-deckers and large single-deckers as most fleets were well stocked with modern vehicles. A switch to high-frequency minibus services in many areas led to thousands of van- and light-truck-derived vehicles being bought from 1984/5 onwards. Deregulation prompted some major operators, notably Greater Manchester, to reduce their fleets and sell relatively modern buses on the secondhand market. Some operators refurbished older vehicles rather than buy new. It took until the early 1990s for the industry to begin to re-equip with large numbers of newer vehicles — and there is a much more widespread use of single-deckers than before. Since 1993, there has been a steady swing over to more accessible lowfloor buses, first with single-deckers and more recently with double-deckers.

The coach market has also changed, with the lightweights of the 1970s mostly being replaced by heavy duty coaches built by foreign-based manufacturers.

The upheavals among operators were paralleled by a shake-out of bus and coach manufacturers. Leyland Bus is no more — slimmed down, sold to Volvo in 1988 and effectively shut down four years later. Dennis has grown into a dominant force, with it and Volvo between them supplying nearly three-quarters of the market. Optare, formed to take over Leyland's Roe plant, moved into complete vehicle building when MCW closed down. German manufacturers Mercedes-Benz and MAN are beginning to increase their sales to the major bus groups.

Among bodybuilders, Plaxton and Wright have become major players in the bus sector, with Plaxton buying Northern Counties in 1995. Spanish coachbuilders are following Belgian, Dutch and German counterparts into the British coach market.

These developments help explain the mix of old and new buses and coaches described in the pages that follow. Inevitably, there isn't space to include some of the rarest and oldest, but I've endeavoured to include details of the vast majority of types still running, together with indications of some of the places you can expect to see them.

GLOSSARY

The following notes may help you make more sense of terms used in the book.

HOW IS A BUS BUILT?

Traditionally, it had a separate **chassis** (the frame in which engine, gearbox, axles and wheels are mounted) and **body** (the upper structure in which passengers travel). These would often be built in separate factories, often hundreds of miles apart. **Integral** or **chassis-less** construction is more common now, with the body and chassis being a single structure in which mechanical units are mounted. **Semi-integral** designs are a halfway house, with a separate **underframe** for the mechanical unit but depending on the body to provide some of the strength.

Engines are mounted in either a **vertical** or **horizontal** position. Vertical engines are mounted either **longitudinally** (front to back in line with the length of the vehicle) at the front, in the middle under the floor (hence, **underfloor** engine) or at the side; or **transversely** (across the width of the chassis) at the rear. **Transmission** (the gearbox and its method of control by the driver) is either **manual** (clutch and floor-mounted gearlever like most cars), **automatic** (two pedals and switch or push-button controls) or **semi-automatic** (two pedals and ability to select all gears). Most manual gearboxes are **synchromesh**.

IS IT A BUS OR A COACH?

A **bus** is designed for local services. Its seats are more robust than luxurious (although many new designs have individual rather than bench-type seats), its doors may be wider, its floor may be nearer the ground and there will be provision for some standing passengers. **Lowfloor** buses have no steps in their entrance or ahead of the rear axle; the previous standard of urban bus is now referred to as **step-entrance** or **standard floor**, but the rapid introduction of lowfloor buses means that they are fast becoming the standard.

A **coach** is a more luxurious vehicle for longer journeys, probably with reclining seats, possibly a toilet, galley and larger windows. **Dual-purpose** or **semi-coaches** usually look like buses from the outside but have coach features inside, but sometimes are coaches modified for interurban bus work. In the context of coaches, **low floors** refer to 3.2m-high vehicles which still have steps leading into the seating area.

DIMENSIONS AND DESCRIPTIONS

These are governed by Construction and Use regulations. The maximum permitted width has recently been increased from 2.5m (8ft 2½in) to 2.55m (8ft 4½in); maximum length is 12m (39ft 4in) except on articulated buses and coaches which can be up to 18m (59ft) long. Two-axle vehicles are limited to a gross weight (vehicle, passengers and luggage) of 17 tonnes; the three-axle gross weight limit is 26 tonnes. The most common sizes of buses today reflect former upper limits of lengths and widths. Double-deckers grew from 27ft to 30ft in the mid-1950s, then to 9.5m, 10m, 11m and occasionally to 12m. Single-deck buses and coaches range from 8.5m to 12m, with 12m the most common length of coaches. There are moves to legalise 15m coaches, but this is unlikely to happen for some years.

It is becoming increasingly difficult to separate minibuses, midibuses and full-size vehicles. **Minibuses**, most converted from vans and light trucks, seat up to around 25 passengers. **Midibuses** used to bridge the gap to 10m single-deckers, but the development of larger Dennis Darts and Volvo B6s has taken midibuses up to 11m. For the purposes of this book, the minibus section deals with truck- and van-derived vehicles and purpose-designed smaller vehicles with their front axle ahead of the entrance door.

Double-deckers are either **highbridge** (around 14ft 6in, maybe taller) or **lowheight** (around 13ft 8in to fit under low bridges). Single-deck coaches range between 3m and 3.7m high usually; double-deck coaches are either 4m high (for international work) or 4.2m. There also are 4m-high half-deck coaches with a lower rear saloon for about 12 passengers.

Passenger doors are **front entrances** where fitted ahead of the front axle, **forward entrances** when directly behind the front axle and **dual-doored** where there are separate entrances and exits. Most buses have two-, three- or four-leaf folding doors; coaches either have hinged or **plug** doors which open to lie with the inner section against the body side and close tight to seal out draughts. Some coaches have an extra offside **Continental** door for nearside access in mainland Europe or on one-way streets in Britain; they may also have a sliding **péage** window in the nearside door so Continental motorway tolls can be paid without opening the door.

Side windows have either **direct** or **bonded glazing** (fixed by adhesive and providing extra strength) or **gasket glazing** (fixed by rubber section and more easily replaced). Windscreens are either **curved** or **flat**. If curved in one plane only, windscreens are **barrel-shaped** when the curve is from top to bottom; if curved in two planes, they are **double-curvature**. **Vee-shaped** screens use two flat planes set at an angle. **BET** (British Electric Traction) companies (absorbed into the National Bus Company in 1969) pioneered a two-section double-curvature windscreen which remains popular today.

The term **window bays** for side windows can be confusing. On double-deckers, convention has it that this refers to the number of lower deck windows, plus centre doors and staircase panels in the main section, but excluding the front and rear overhang. So a bus with six windows on the upper deck has a four-bay body. On single-deckers, it refers to the number of windows behind the driver's cab.

Should you have comments on how to improve *abc Bus & Coach Recognition*, please write to the Publishing Editor, Ian Allan Publishing Ltd, Riverdene Business Park, Molesey Road, Hersham, Surrey, KT12 4RG.

Alan Millar
Glasgow, 1998

LEFT: Setra: A French-built S215 Rational coach with gasket glazing. German-built Setras are at the top of the price range, and this cheaper model was imported to broaden the appeal of the integral Setra coach range (see page 134).

Part 1. DOUBLE-DECK BUSES

CHASSIS AND INTEGRALS

Most British double-deckers have transverse rear engines and an entrance ahead of the front axle (and sometimes a separate exit door directly behind the front axle or somewhere ahead of the rear axle). This design was pioneered in 1958 with the Leyland Atlantean and these buses have all but eliminated traditional front-engined half-cab models with the cab and engine over the front axle and either a rear entrance on an open platform or a forward entrance behind folding or sliding doors directly behind the front axle. The last half-cabs were built in 1968 and this style of bus is now confined largely to the busiest routes through central London. The Atlantean layout has been challenged periodically since 1973, notably by the now disappearing front-engined Volvo Ailsa, designed as an answer to problems with early rear-engined designs; by the underfloor-engined Volvo Citybus and Leyland Lion and various longitudinal rear-engined products from Dennis and Scania. The move to lowfloor double-deckers seems to be strengthening the hold of the transverse rear-engined chassis.

AEC Routemaster

Built: Southall, Middlesex 1958-68
Engines: AEC AV590, AV690; Leyland O.600; Cummins C-Series; Iveco 8360; Scania DS9-9TA; DAF 11.6 litre
Transmission: AEC fully and semi-automatic
Main areas of operation: London, Reading

The Routemaster is probably the most widely recognised bus in Britain. It's also the last traditional half-cab double-decker that you're likely to see in all-day service. It was designed by London Transport in close co-operation with AEC and Park Royal, west London chassis and bodybuilders who merged with Leyland in 1962, and owes its survival to its robust, corrosion-resistant aluminium integral body. The Routemaster's independent front suspension, hydraulic brakes and (on most survivors) automatic transmission were advanced features on a 1950s bus.

Of the 2,875 that were built, all but 115 were ordered by LT and over 600 were still operating the busiest weekday services in the capital in 1998. Although they cannot go on for ever, route contracts will assure the survival of at least some until 2003. Most surviving London Routemasters are 72-seat 30ft-long RML-class models identifiable by an extra, shorter window halfway along both decks, but there still are over 100 of the original 27ft 6in-long 64-seat RM class models with four equal-length windows on the bottom deck. Reading Mainline, the principal Routemaster operator outside London, uses ex-LT RM-class vehicles. Rarer types are: RMC and RCL, 57- and 65-seat versions of the RM and RML built originally for Green Line coach services and fitted with enclosed rear platforms; forward-entrance short (RMA) and long (RMF) models built respectively for British European Airways and Northern General Transport; and 10 ERM-class 32ft 6in open-top 76-seaters operated by Arriva in London and created in

1990 by fitting sections from scrapped buses into standard RMs. Dorset-based Shaftesbury & District has similarly lengthened an RMA.

Most of the London RMs and RMLs were fitted with new Cummins and Iveco engines in the early 1990s, replacing their worn-out AEC and Leyland units, and many have had their bodies refurbished. One London vehicle was fitted with a DAF engine and, more recently, Go Ahead had 38 London Central RMs fitted with downrated Scania engines.

The Routemaster's low bonnet and grille give drivers a good view of the kerbside. The vertically-divided grille usually has a triangular AEC/LT badge at the top.

ABOVE: *AEC Routemaster: The most common type of Routemaster still running is the 72-seat RML with short middle bay on both decks. The first 24 were built in 1961-2, with 500 following between 1965 and 1968. This 1966 example is one of 24 leased by London Transport to Kentish Bus to operate route 19 and painted in the operator's then livery of maroon and cream. These were among the Routemasters repowered with Iveco 8360 engines. Kentish Bus is now called Arriva Kent Thameside and its London routes have been transferred to Arriva's fleets in the capital. The sliding cab door is open on this bus.*

LEFT: *AEC Routemaster: Mobile and static London landmarks. Rear view of two 64-seat RMs approaching Big Ben. This shows the open platforms which once were a common feature on almost all double-deckers in Britain and which have remained popular in London because they speed boarding and alighting. This photograph was taken before the London Buses subsidiaries were privatised; London General, which still operates route 11, is now part of Go Ahead.*

ABOVE: *AEC Routemaster: London Coaches, formerly part of London Buses and now owned by Arriva, created the ERM class of open-toppers — with their exceptionally long wheelbase — by adding an extra body bay to some early RM-type Routemasters. This turned them into 76-seaters, with 44 seats upstairs; the economics of double-deck sightseeing buses in London demand vehicles with the highest possible top deck capacity, as tourists rarely ride downstairs. On this vehicle, the sliding cab door has been closed.*

Bristol VRT

Built: Bristol 1968-81
Engines: Gardner 6LX, 6LXB, 6LXC;
Leyland 501, 680
Transmission: Self-Changing Gears
semi- and fully-automatic
Bodywork: ECW, Alexander, East
Lancs, Northern Counties,
Willowbrook, MCW
Main areas of operation: Throughout
Britain, especially England

The Bristol VRT was the last of the first generation of rear-engined double-deckers to be launched and was developed primarily for state-owned operators which, until 1965, were the only customers Bristol and ECW were permitted to supply. Several of the 4,474 built are still operated by former National Bus Company fleets; most are 9.5m-long Series 3 models with ECW bodies. The VRT has a front radiator and the engine compartment is usually enclosed entirely by the bodywork. Series 1 and 2 models built until 1974 have cooling vents around the engine compartment, while the Series 3 models built from 1974 has enclosed engine compartments with cooling vents located to the rear of the bodywork, below the upper deck windows.

RIGHT TOP: *Bristol VRT: Front offside view of an ECW-bodied Series 3 working for Solent Blueline in Southampton, but in the livery of the operator's parent Southern Vectis fleet on the Isle of Wight. Note one of the air intakes below the short rearmost side window; a second wraps round the nearside corner. Compare the position of the lower deck side windows with the highbridge ECW body shown on page 36.*

DAF DB250

Built: Eindhoven, Netherlands 1991 to date
Engine: DAF RS 8.65-litre
Transmission: ZF or Voith automatic
Bodywork: Optare, Alexander, Northern Counties
Main areas of operation: London, Reading, Eastbourne, Birmingham, Bristol, Manchester, Poole, Salisbury, Southampton, Dundee

Following the closure of Metro-Cammell Weymann in 1989, DAF Bus bought the rights to the design of MCW's Metrobus chassis and incorporated its rear axle and suspension and transverse engine layout into the 9.9m DB250 which was developed for the British market, but has also been sold in Turkey. Many of the chassis parts come from DAF's SB220 single-decker. A 10.4m lowfloor version — the first lowfloor double-decker on the market — was launched in October 1997. Both models have rear radiators with offside grilles in the engine compartment.

LEFT: *DAF DB250: Rear view of two lowfloor DB250s with Optare Spectra bodies, delivered in 1998 to Bullock's of Cheadle.*

13

Dennis Dominator, Dragon

Built: Guildford, Surrey 1977-96
Engines: Gardner 6LXB, 5LXC,
6LXCT, LG1200; Rolls-Royce Eagle;
DAF; Cummins L10
Transmission: Voith, ZF or Maxwell
automatic
Bodywork: Alexander, East Lancs,
Marshall, Northern Counties,
Willowbrook, Duple Metsec
Main areas of operation: South
Yorkshire, east London, Surrey,
Bournemouth, Chester, Hull, Leicester,
Greater Manchester, Swindon,
Warrington, Grimsby

The Dominator was Dennis's first UK bus chassis for 10 years and helped establish the marque in many fleets which never bought it before. Although earlier models (including 11m single-deckers built between 1978 and 1980) have been sold by their original owners, many double-deckers still operate with Mainline which, as South Yorkshire Transport, bought 450 with Rolls-Royce engines. Capital Citybus (part of FirstGroup) and some Arriva subsidiaries operate Dominators in London and Surrey. The Dominator has a front radiator, provision for the engine compartment to be fully enclosed — where it is not, thick body panels conceal the engine cooling ducts — and it has cooling grilles at the sides, directly above the engine compartment.

The six-wheel Dragon (and Condor when bought by China Motor Bus) was developed from the Dominator for the Hong Kong market and sold in significantly greater volumes than the Dominator. A batch of 20, with locally assembled Duple Metsec kit bodies, went to Stagecoach's Kenya subsidiary

BELOW: Dennis Dominator: Nearside rear view of a 10m Dominator operated by Mainline in Sheffield. This shows the semi-bustle effect created when the engine compartment isn't completely enclosed by the bodywork. This also shows the 10m Alexander RH body with short middle bay like the RML Routemaster.

in 1995/6 and was transferred to Stagecoach Manchester in 1998 for some of the city's busiest services. When new, these had up to 115 seats but around 20 seats were removed for UK operation. Duple Metsec is a Dennis subsidiary based in the West Midlands.

Dennis Falcon V

Built: Guildford, Surrey 1981-4
Engine: Mercedes-Benz OM421 V6
Transmission: Voith automatic
Bodywork: East Lancs, Northern Counties
Main areas of operation: Fife, Bedford

The 10.5m long Falcon V — the 'V' denotes its vee-formation engine — was an unsuccessful attempt by Dennis to sell a double-decker that was 10% cheaper, 10% lighter and carried 10% more passengers than rival models. The compact engine is mounted longitudinally at the back, partly under a raised floor. Only six were built. An East Lancs-bodied prototype became a playbus in Stevenage, two 88-seat East Lancs-bodied two-door models went to Nottingham City Transport and were modified to gain front radiators, but were sold on to Cedar Coaches of Bedford for schools transport. Three Northern Counties-bodied 84-seaters with rear radiators went to Greater Manchester Transport in 1984 and have since been sold to Rennie's of Dunfermline. Additionally, 10 Falcon Vs were built as 12m single-deck coaches with Perkins V8 engines and Duple bodies.

BELOW: *Dennis Falcon V: Rear view of one of the three Northern Counties-bodied Falcon Vs built for Greater Manchester PTE, with a longer rear overhang (and extra window second from back upstairs) when compared with standard 9.5m double-deckers bought for that same fleet.*

Dennis Arrow

Built: Guildford, Surrey 1996-8
Engine: Cummins 6CT
Transmission: ZF automatic
Bodywork: East Lancs, Northern Counties
Main areas of operation: London, Surrey, Nottingham, Liverpool

Like the Falcon V, the Arrow is 10.5m long and has a longitudinal engine. It is a shorter version of the Lance single-decker and, like it, has a rear radiator. By 1998, when the advent of lowfloor double-deckers appeared to have ended its short production life, 75 had been sold — 56 to Capital Citybus. Other customers were Nottingham, London & Country, London Traveller, Aintree Coachlines (whose first Arrow carries Lance badging) and — ironically in view of the Falcon V's fate — two to playbus associations in Suffolk.

BELOW: Dennis Arrow: It's interesting to compare the different approaches to a similar concept to the Falcon V 12 years on, in this 1986 Arrow with Northern Counties Palatine II body.

Dennis Trident

Built: Guildford, Surrey from 1998
Engine: Cummins 6CT
Transmission: ZF or Voith automatic
Bodywork: Alexander, East Lancs, Plaxton
Main areas of operation: London, Oxford, Nottingham

The 2.55m-wide Trident, available in 9.9m and 10.4m lengths, is Dennis's lowfloor double-deck chassis designed primarily for London and expected to start entering service early in 1999. It is derived from the six-wheel Trident built for Hong Kong, but whereas the export model has a longitudinally-mounted Cummins M11 engine, the four-wheel British model has a very compact transverse-mounted 6CT, a layout that keeps the rear overhang as short as possible and allows the back seat to be placed over the engine. Impressive pre-launch orders were placed for over 200, including 100 for Stagecoach East London and others for Oxford Bus and Nottingham.

ABOVE: *Dennis Trident: Artist's impression of a two-axle Trident with London-specification lowfloor Alexander ALX400 body.* **Dennis**

Iveco TurboCity

Built: Valle Uffita, Italy 1991
Engine: Iveco 8460.21
Transmission: ZF automatic
Bodywork: Alexander
Main area of operation: North Devon

Iveco — Fiat's commercial vehicle division — has a long-term plan to sell citybuses in Britain, but its initial efforts were unsuccessful and it is currently waiting until a European Union directive on bus design is agreed before it is prepared to have another attempt.

In 1991, it brought its TurboCity-U — a popular vehicle with Italian city fleets — to Britain and had a 10.7m Alexander RH-type 83-seat double-deck body fitted on the first chassis. Unlike standard R-types, it was fitted with flat windscreens to the design used on Italian single-deck citybuses. The solitary prototype was bought by Filer's of Ilfracombe and operates regularly along the North Devon coast, linking its home resort with Barnstaple and Westward Ho!

LEFT: *Iveco TurboCity: The solitary TurboCity double-decker, with Italian citybus windscreens on its Alexander RH body, in Ilfracombe.*

Leyland Atlantean

Built: Leyland, Lancashire 1958-84
Engine: Leyland O.600, 680, 690

Transmission: Leyland semi- and fully-automatic; Voith automatic
Bodywork: Alexander, East Lancs, ECW, MCW, Marshall, Northern Counties, Park Royal, Roe, Willowbrook

ABOVE: *Leyland Atlantean: One of the last deliveries of AN68C Atlanteans to Nottingham. Note the engine cooling on the nearside and also by louvres on the top of the centre section of the bonnet. This shows the rear-end treatment of this operator's unusual Northern Counties body, with five bays, a tall lower deck reversing window (a standard feature on contemporary East Lancs bodies) and a narrow entrance door. Nottingham's design began to evolve in the mid-1960s and met the operator's desire to standardise on replacement body parts and provide as many seats as possible on the bottom deck.*

Main areas of operation: Throughout Britain, but principal survivors are in Edinburgh, Manchester, Liverpool, Leeds, Nottingham, Southampton, Preston and Plymouth

This is the bus that changed the shape of British double-deckers. All classes of operator bought the Atlantean over its long production run and, although it is fast disappearing from major fleets, many still operate in places like Merseyside and Greater Manchester where some of the last were supplied. The original PDR model was replaced by the AN68 Atlantean in 1972 and these have either an offside-only or both offside and nearside grilles on the three-section engine compartment; the radiator is behind the offside grille. Most have bustle cutaway-effect bodywork above the engine compartment, but bodybuilders sometimes fitted side fairings to reduce the cutaway to the area above the centre of the engine cover. Fishwick of Leyland has two prototype AN69 chassis with turbocharged 690 engines; one has the same 'quiet pack' engine covers as the B20 Fleetlines described below.

Leyland (Daimler) Fleetline

Built: Coventry, 1960-73; Leyland, Lancashire 1973-80
Engines: Gardner 6LX, 6LXB; Leyland 680, 690; Iveco 8361
Transmission: Self-Changing Gears semi- and fully-automatic
Bodywork: Alexander, East Lancs, MCW, ECW, Northern Counties, Park Royal, Roe, Willowbrook
Main areas of operation (principal survivors): London, Greater Manchester, Dundee, Derby, Southend

The first original generation rear-engined double-decker to go out of production, the Fleetline is disappearing even more quickly from our streets. In the late 1960s, it was Britain's best-selling double-decker, partly because it was the first in its class to be available with lowheight bodywork. Between 1970 and 1978, London Transport bought 2,646, but engineering problems prompted the sale of most of them by the mid-1980s and none now run with any of the major London operators. The Fleetline was rebadged as a Leyland product from the end of 1974.

All Fleetlines have an engine

RIGHT: *Leyland Fleetline: Offside rear view of a standard specification Fleetline in the Busways (former Tyne & Wear PTE) fleet before it was taken over by Stagecoach. This also shows the panoramic window version of the Alexander AL body*

compartment radiator, fitted on the offside on standard models, behind a vertically-slatted grille and in an engine cover with a single opening section. They have bustle cutaway-effect bodywork above the engine compartment, but some — including the first 2,246 London buses — were built with side fairings. The final 400 London Fleetlines, coded B20 by Leyland, were designed to be quieter and are identifiable by a completely different engine cover design, with two sloping ventilator chimneys above the engine — that on the offside being wider; 200 of these had their original Leyland 690 turbocharged engines replaced by Italian-built Iveco diesels and were then fitted with an additional nearside grille.

ABOVE: *Leyland Fleetline B20: Rear view of a Park Royal-bodied B20 Fleetline, new to London Transport and sold to one of the sightseeing operators. The offside ventilation chimney is wider than the one on the nearside. MCW built similar bodies on London Fleetlines and other contemporary vehicles; they have a smaller top deck emergency door and have more pronounced guttering above the offside rear emergency door downstairs.*

Leyland Titan

Built: Park Royal, London 1978-80 (prototypes built 1975-7), Workington, Cumbria 1981-4
Engines: Gardner 6LXB, 6LXCT; Leyland TL11 (501 in prototypes)
Transmission: Leyland fully-automatic
Bodywork: Park Royal, Leyland
Main areas of operation: London, Reading, Sussex, Swindon, Gloucester, Scotland, Teesside, Cambridge, Liverpool

The highbridge Titan TN15 (reviving a Leyland model name used from 1927 to 1969) was meant to be Leyland's standard double-decker for the 1980s. It was developed in the early 1970s using lessons learned from the first generation of rear-engined double-deckers and, like the Routemaster, was bestowed with features requested by London Transport — like integral construction, independent front suspension, hydraulic brakes and, to achieve better engine cooling, a separately-located radiator compartment above the engine. It took longer than planned to put it into production, by which time less complex competitors had appeared on the market, so far fewer were built than Leyland had hoped. London Transport and Reading were its only long-term customers, with LT buying 1,164 and five from West Midlands PTE, while Reading took 12, 10 of them motorway express buses with Gardner 6LXCT engines. The only other significant batch, 15 for Greater Manchester, was sold in the mid-1980s. The London fleet was rebuilt with air brakes and is steadily being distributed secondhand around the country; on privatisation, most were acquired by Stagecoach and Go Ahead and many Stagecoach Titans have been transferred to other group fleets.

Titans all have barrel-shaped windscreens to London Transport design and have deep lower deck side windows. They are most distinguishable at the back by their asymmetric window arrangement above the engine compartment; the radiator is in the offside area above the engine compartment.

LEFT: Leyland Titan: One of Reading's first Titans, showing the front and offside treatment of two-door models; on the few built new with one door and a forward staircase, the short window above the front wheel on this bus is fitted instead ahead of the two main lower deck windows.

RIGHT: Leyland Titan: Nearside rear view of an ex-London Titan operating with Stagecoach in Glasgow. Note the asymmetrical rear end and the style of upper deck emergency door also found on early ECW and Roe-bodied Olympians.

Leyland Olympian

Built: Bristol 1980-3 (prototypes built 1978/9); Workington, Cumbria 1983-93
Engines: Gardner 6LXB, 6LXCT, 5LXCT, LG1200; Leyland TL11; Cummins L10
Transmission: Leyland semi- or fully-automatic, Voith, ZF or Maxwell automatic
Bodywork: Leyland, Alexander, East Lancs, ECW, Marshall, Northern Counties, Optare, Roe
Main areas of operation: Throughout Britain (notably London, Edinburgh, Glasgow, Aberdeen, Dundee, Newcastle, Liverpool, Manchester, Leeds, Bradford, Hull, Bristol, Cardiff, Swansea, Preston, Derby, Nottingham, Blackpool, Birmingham, Swindon, Bournemouth, Oxford, Luton, Cambridge, Reading, Norwich, Southend, Isle of Wight, Isle of Man)

Although conceived as a lowheight Titan, to be supplied to customers of independent bodybuilders which might not otherwise buy a Leyland, the Olympian became its standard double-decker and by far the best-selling chassis in its class with sales of over 5,000 at home and abroad. It has less sophisticated air suspension than the Titan, as well as air brakes and a simpler cooling system with a front radiator. The engine compartment, with cooling ducts from the rear and upper deck sides, is totally enclosed on most buses or within thick body sides as on some Dennis Dominators. It was built in 9.6m, 10m, 11m and three-axle 12m lengths, although the only UK customer for the 12m version was Stagecoach which bought three. Latterly, most Olympians had Cummins engines and ZF gearboxes. The Leyland Olympian was superseded by a Volvo version from 1993.

BELOW: Leyland Olympian: Offside rear view of an Optare-bodied Olympian supplied to Reading Buses in 1988. The body is to standard ECW design and has the large rear upper deck emergency door fitted on most of these bodies.

Leyland Lion

Built: Silkeborg, Denmark 1986-8
Engine: Leyland TL11H
Transmission: ZF automatic
Bodywork: Alexander, East Lancs, Northern Counties
Main areas of operation: Nottingham, Edinburgh, Chester, Gloucester

The Lion was Leyland's answer to Volvo's mid-engined Citybus — a vehicle with even weight distribution and less complex driveline, but a higher floor than rear-engined models. It was developed from the standard horizontal-engined single-deck underframe produced by DAB, Leyland's then subsidiary in Denmark and now part of Scania, and was withdrawn from the market after Volvo bought Leyland Bus. Only 32 were built, 19 with Alexander bodies for the Scottish Bus Group and 13 for Nottingham. Some of the SBG vehicles were sold after privatisation to Chester City Transport and independent operator Cottrell of Mitcheldean. The Lion has a front radiator and a slightly higher floor than the Volvo.

ABOVE: Leyland Lion: A Nottingham City Transport Lion, with the operator's non-standard design of six-bay Northern Counties body; the top deck windscreen and roof dome treatment is closer to East Lancs style. Nottingham specified sliding cab doors on its Lions and Volvo Citybuses.

MCW Metrobus

Built: Birmingham 1978-89
Engines: Gardner 6LXB; Rolls-Royce Eagle; Cummins L10
Transmission: Voith automatic
Bodywork: MCW, Alexander, Northern Counties
Main areas of operation: London, West Midlands, Glasgow, Dundee, Newcastle, Merseyside, Greater Manchester, West and South Yorkshire, Bristol, Hull, Leicester, Reading, Canterbury

Having built the Scania-based Metropolitan from 1973 to 1978 (of which extremely few survive now),

ABOVE: *MCW Metrobus: A Mk1 Metrobus new to South Yorkshire PTE and operated by Mainline, which took over the PTE's bus services in 1986 and became part of FirstGroup in 1998. Note the asymmetrical lower deck windscreen.*

Metro-Cammell Weymann turned itself into a complete vehicle builder by launching the Metrobus with its own chassis, a British engine and a German gearbox. MCW's courage in launching it with little development was rewarded by healthy initial orders, especially after Leyland suspended Titan production in 1980/1. London Transport bought over 1,400 and West Midlands over 1,100.

In its initial form, the highbridge MCW bodywork (with which most

were fitted) was most distinguished by an asymmetrical windscreen carried over from the discontinued Metropolitan. Its radiator is in the offside of the engine compartment, but there also is a front grille, painted black on earlier models when they were new. Most London Metrobuses were to this design.

The Mk2 body was launched in 1982 with 60% fewer body parts. It was cheaper to build and differs most

RIGHT: *MCW Metrobus: Front and rear views of Mk2 Metrobuses in Reading. This shows the flat windscreen version.*

markedly at the front where it has a peaked roof dome, a shallower symmetrical windscreen with either barrel-shaped or flat glass and more heavily moulded front panels and grille. When new, the pillars between the side windows were wider and there was a much larger glass area on the upper deck

rear emergency door, but refurbished West Midlands and Mainline vehicles have lost some of these distinguishing features.

Metrobus underframes were also bodied by Alexander and Northern Counties.

Scania N112/N113

Built: Katrineholm, Sweden 1980 to date

Engine: Scania DS11

Transmission: Voith or Scania automatic

Bodywork: Alexander, Northern Counties, East Lancs, Marshall

Main areas of operation: London, West Midlands, Leicester, Newcastle, Merseyside, Greater Manchester, West Yorkshire, Hull, Cardiff, Newport, Brighton, Nottingham

Scania first supplied the British double-deck market in a joint venture with MCW, fitting its BR111 running units into the Metropolitan. When that arrangement ended, it developed its own double-deck chassis based around the CR112 single-decker to create a vehicle known initially as the BR112, but which soon became the N112; it was replaced by the N113 when chassis changes were introduced and is likely to be changed again if Scania offers a lowfloor double-decker in Britain. The Metropolitan had a Scania gearbox and offside and nearside radiators, but the N112 and N113 have just one offside radiator, ahead of the rear axle, and most have Voith gearboxes.

BELOW: *Scania N113: The offside grille ahead of the rear axle is a distinguishing feature of the Scania N-Series, as is the manufacturer's treatment of the side engine covers. This Brighton & Hove example has an East Lancs four-bay body with curved top deck windscreen and BET driver's windscreen.*

It took a long time for the N112 to be accepted by pro-British public sector bus buyers and, for a long time, only Newport bought them regularly, but deregulation and privatisation boosted sales in the late 1980s and early 1990s.

Scania K92

Built: Katrineholm, Sweden 1987

Engine: Scania DS9

Transmission: Scania CAG synchromesh

Bodywork: East Lancs

Main areas of operation: London, Hampshire

The longitudinally-engined K92 (K93 from 1988) sold mainly as a coach or single-deck bus in the UK, but four 11.2m chassis were fitted with high-capacity East Lancs double-deck bodies in 1987 and supplied to Maidstone Boro'line and Grey Green. All had CAG, a computer-controlled transmission based on a synchromesh gearbox. Air intakes to the 9-litre engine are on the nearside, behind the rear axle, and at the back. When the Maidstone company folded in 1992, its two buses were bought by Oakley, a Hampshire coach operator, for school contracts.

ABOVE: *Scania K92: One of two East Lancs-bodied K92 double-deckers built for Maidstone Boro'line and sold to a Hampshire operator. Apart from their sheer length, they are also identifiable by the grilles around the nearside rear and back end.*

Volvo Ailsa B55

Built: Irvine, Ayrshire 1973-84

Engine: Volvo TD70

Transmission: Self-Changing Gears semi- and fully-automatic; Allison and Voith automatic.

Bodywork: Alexander, East Lancs, Northern Counties, Marshall

Main areas of operation: Glasgow, Dundee, Fife, Cardiff

The front-engined, Scottish-designed Ailsa was developed by Volvo's British importer soon after traditional half-cab designs ceased to be available and when some operators felt rear-engined buses were unreliable. Its semi-integral underframe has a compact yet powerful 6.7-litre engine fitted in the overhang between the driver's cab and the front entrance. On most Ailsas, the staircase runs forward from behind the cab, leaving space for only one seat at the front of the top deck. Standard models are 9.8m long with up to 79 seats, but Travel Dundee has 10.3m 84-seaters. The main identification points are a three-leaf entrance door which folds forward to clear the space around the engine compartment, an offside cab door (either hinged or sliding) and a large front radiator grille that hinges up for engine access.

LEFT: Volvo Ailsa B55: A Travel Dundee Ailsa, with Alexander AV-type body and hinged cab door, still showing the operator's former name of Tayside Buses. Most AV bodies had peaked domes.

Volvo Citybus

Built: Irvine, Ayrshire 1982-86, 1997 to date; Borås, Sweden, 1987-93
Engine: Volvo THD100, 101, DH10
Transmission: Voith or ZF automatic
Bodywork: Alexander, East Lancs, Northern Counties, Marshall
Main areas of operation: London, Manchester, Glasgow, Nottingham, Edinburgh, Fife, Bournemouth, Bristol, Northampton, Derby, Burnley, Cambridge, Colchester

The British-developed Citybus was the first mid underfloor-engined double-decker to go into volume production. It replaced the Ailsa and, over the years, has been designated B10MD and D10M. Originally it combined the running units of the B10M single-decker with a perimeter underframe similar to that on the Ailsa, reducing the number of unique parts for Volvo's double-decker and appealing to a wider range of customers in the years before Leyland was taken over. Later vehicles were virtually standard B10M chassis. Demand tailed off after that, with none built after Northampton Transport bought six in 1993 until Nottingham City Transport bought 10 with nearside radiators in 1997. Others have front radiators, sometimes concealed behind an Ailsa-sized grille and, just to confuse the unwary, some East Lancs-bodied Citybuses have offside cab doors like the Ailsa.

ABOVE: *Volvo Citybus: Yellow Coaches, part of the council-owned Bournemouth fleet, is the operator of this East Lancs-bodied Citybus with high-backed coach seats. The mix of BET driver's windscreen and double-curvature top deck windscreen is one of many permutations further described in the bodywork section.*

Volvo Olympian

Built: Irvine, Ayrshire 1993 to date
Engines: Volvo TD102, D10A;
Cummins L10, M11
Transmission: ZF or Voith automatic
Bodywork: Alexander, East Lancs,
Northern Counties, Plaxton
Main areas of operation: Throughout
Britain (notably London, Edinburgh,
Glasgow, Aberdeen, Dundee,
Newcastle, Liverpool, Manchester,
Leeds, Bradford, Hull, Bristol, Preston,
Nottingham, Oxford, Luton,
Cambridge, Isle of Wight)

Volvo transferred Olympian production to the former Ailsa plant at Irvine shortly before closing Leyland Bus's last remaining chassis manufacturing facility at Workington. As well as rebadging it as a Volvo, it was given Volvo hubs, brakes and electrics, the Gardner engine and Voith gearbox options were dropped and, although the Cummins L10 engine remained available initially, Volvo's 9.6-litre engine became standard. The L10 ceased to be offered from 1996 when Euro 2 emission standards were introduced, but at least one M11 has been fitted experimentally in a Lothian Olympian. However, Voith gearboxes are now fitted as an option. Visually, the main distinguishing features of the Volvo Olympian are its badges and, when fitted, front wheel rings.

In October 1997, Volvo showed what it called a concept chassis for a lowfloor double-decker at the Coach & Bus Show in Birmingham. This had a longitudinally-mounted nearside engine, thought to be a D7 or D8 diesel, and was assumed to be a successor to the Olympian. However, this will be superseded by something more closely resembling the transverse-engined Olympian when Volvo enters the lowfloor double-deck market in 1999.

LEFT: Volvo Olympian: Badging is the main difference on the Volvo version of the best-selling Olympian. This one, in London & Country (now part of Arriva) livery, has an East Lancs E-type body.

ABOVE: Volvo: Detail of the nearside rear of the prototype lowfloor double-decker, with longitudinal engine and Plaxton President body which was exhibited in October 1997.

BODYWORK

Alexander AL-type

Built: Falkirk, Stirlingshire
Height: High
Chassis: Leyland Atlantean, Fleetline, Bristol VRT
Main areas of operation: Aberdeen, Edinburgh, Liverpool, Preston, Bournemouth, Northampton, Cardiff

prefix to denote the use of aluminium alloy, rather than steel framing. So the AL is an alloy-framed L-type. All versions have equal depth windows on both decks, with an extra short window at the top deck rear on 10m models. There are many variations — short bays or panoramic windows of double the length (sometimes both together where weakened panoramic window bodies have been rebuilt); curved or flat windscreens; rounded or peaked roof domes (Northampton bought VRTs with peaked front domes and rounded rear ones); side engine fairings or full bustle. MTL has inherited Merseyside PTE's

ABOVE: *Alexander AL: Offside and front nearside view of short-window AL bodies on Leyland Fleetlines in the Yellow Buses Bournemouth fleet. Some AL bodies have peaked domes similar to those on the AV-bodied Ailsa shown on page 27.*

Alexander, now the world's largest producer of double-deck bus bodies, built the AL-type between 1972 and 1982 for a growing base of customers throughout Britain. The company identified its models by single letter codes introduced in 1961, initially with double-deckers starting from 'A' and single-deckers starting backwards from 'Z', but around 1970 added an 'A'

surviving AL-type Atlanteans with metal rather than rubber window surrounds. VRTs have large front grilles; the front mouldings on Atlantean and Fleetline bodies varied over the years. AL-type design features were fitted in the AV-type body built exclusively on early Volvo Ailsas (see page 27).

Alexander R-type and Royale

Built: Falkirk, Stirlingshire; Mallusk, Co Antrim
Height: High and low
Chassis: Dennis Dominator; Iveco TurboCity; Leyland Lion; Leyland and Volvo Olympian; Volvo Citybus and Ailsa; MCW Metrobus; Scania N112, N113
Main areas of operation: Much of urban Britain, including London, Scotland, Birmingham, Newcastle, Liverpool, Preston, Bournemouth, Northampton, Cardiff, Sheffield, West Yorkshire, Hull, Leicester, Nottingham, Newport, Oxford, Bristol, Northampton, Grimsby, Bedford, Cambridge, Portsmouth

The R-type, introduced in 1980, is a four-bay body with an extra centre half-bay on 10m models and five bays on Stagecoach's three 12m Olympians. The highbridge RH has deep, equal depth side windows on both decks; the lowheight RL (bought in large quantities by Stagecoach) has shallower, equal depth side windows. Both models have the same deep upper deck windscreens with a pointed effect and a choice of either curved or flat glazing — so the side windows on the RL are shallower than its top deck windscreen. Travel Dundee has Citybuses with separately-mounted front glasses. The driver's windscreen (deeper on some models) can either be flat vee-shaped, flat with quarterlights, curved, or BET-style double-curvature. Ailsas and early Citybuses have a large grille and early Scanias have a plain front dash; later models have small grilles which are either functional or ornamental, depending on the location of the

*BELOW: Alexander RH: A two-door RH-bodied Volvo Olympian operated by Capital Citybus on one of the London Transport routes that requires red buses. The body was built at Mallusk and shows the vee-windscreen treatment. Note that the upper deck windscreen stops fractionally above the side windows upstairs. **Alexander***

radiator. The Mallusk factory builds two-door RH-bodied Olympians for export to Dublin Bus and also for London operators.

In 1993, the R-type was complemented by the Royale, with curved windscreens and lower dash and an option of either square-edged gasket-glazed side windows or full bonded glazing. All Royales have so far been built on Volvo Olympian chassis. In common with recent practice, many R-types and Royales have unglazed back ends so operators can sell the entire space for advertising.

ABOVE: *Alexander RL: A 10m RL-bodied Leyland Olympian with Stagecoach in Portsmouth. Note the BET windscreen and that the upper deck windscreen is deeper than the side windows.*

BELOW: *Alexander Royale: A Yorkshire Coastliner (Blazefield group) highbridge Royale on a Volvo Olympian chassis. Kelvin runs lowheight Royales around Glasgow.* **Alexander**

Alexander ALX400

Built: Falkirk, Stirlingshire

Height: Low

Chassis: Dennis Trident; DAF DB250; Volvo

Main area of operation: London

Alexander's UK market lowfloor double-decker, the ALX400, has been developed as a smaller version of the 12m ALX500 supplied to Hong Kong. Styling of the 2.55m-wide body bears a family resemblance to the Royale, but has the same 'smiling' mouldings below the windscreen as on the ALX200 and 300 single-deckers. Early orders are for DAF DB250s for Arriva fleets and Dennis Tridents for Stagecoach East London.

RIGHT:
Alexander
ALX400: The
10.4m lowfloor
ALX400, on a
DAF chassis
destined for service
with Arriva
Serving London.
Alexander

East Lancs

Built: Blackburn, Lancashire

Height: High and low

Chassis: Dennis Dominator, Falcon V, Arrow; Leyland Atlantean, Fleetline, Olympian; Volvo Citybus, Ailsa, Olympian; Scania N112, N113, K92

Main areas of operation: London, Dundee, Blackburn, Blackpool, Brighton, Birmingham, Liverpool, Preston, Bournemouth, Southampton, Cardiff, Hull, Leicester, Nottingham, Newport, Derby, Ipswich, Plymouth, Warrington, Swindon

Until recently, East Lancs was prepared to build bespoke buses to meet some of its customers' very individual requirements. Because of this, a body style introduced in the early 1960s on rear-engined double-deckers was evolved and updated over the years with several permutations of front windscreens and side window designs.

In its most common form, the five-bay body is relatively square with equal depth windows on both decks. At 10m, it has longer rather than extra bays, but there also are some newer models with four-bay bodies. The upper deck front windows are raked back slightly and many have large upper deck emergency windows and lower deck rear windows. This latter feature, most common on Atlanteans and Fleetlines, is to help drivers when reversing. Front roof domes can be flat, peaked or rounded; upper deck windscreens are either separate flat glasses, flat vertically-divided glasses, one-piece flat or one-piece or divided double-curvature; and drivers' windscreens are either one-piece flat, divided flat, or curved in Alexander style (one-piece or divided). Side windows are usually gasket glazed with either round or square corners, but some (including some particularly bespoke vehicles for Nottingham) have bonded glazing.

A further variant is the E-type body

ABOVE: East Lancs: A five-bay body, typical of hundreds supplied throughout the 1970s, on a Southampton Citybus (now First Citybus) Leyland Atlantean. This has separate upper deck windscreens and an Alexander-style driver's windscreen.

LEFT: East Lancs: A later four-bay body, also for Southampton, on a Dennis Dominator. This has a flat upper deck windscreen and divided Alexander-style driver's windscreen. This is a variation on the designs shown on pages 28 and 25 on the Bournemouth Volvo Citybus and the Brighton & Hove Scania N113.

which, at first glance, looks quite like an Alexander R-type. The first 18 were built in 1984 on South Yorkshire and Leicester Dominators and could only be distinguished from their Alexander counterparts by a ventilation louvre on the staircase panel, in line with the bottom of the lower deck windows, and because their lower deck emergency door window stops short of the tops of the main bay windows. Later versions for other customers have standard East Lancs large upper deck emergency doors and an additional moulding strap between the two decks, a few inches above the lower deck windows. Nottingham City Transport and Stagecoach Kingston upon Hull have E-types with five-bay bodies.

BELOW: East Lancs E-type: The similarity to the Alexander RH is clear on this Yellow Buses Dennis Dominator in Bournemouth. The Alexander original would normally have a deeper vee-shaped driver's windscreen and more elaborate lower front dash; the E-type also has quite different window mountings at the side and a horizontal panel joint which, on this bus, is the lower point of the 'Room inside for 210' side advertisement.

East Lancs Cityzen and Pyoneer

Built: Blackburn, Lancashire
Height: High or low
Chassis: Dennis Arrow; Volvo Citybus, Olympian, rebodied B58; Scania N113
Main areas of operation: London, Newcastle, Manchester, Brighton, Nottingham

The highbridge Cityzen, launched in 1995 exclusively on the Scania N113, was the first of a new range of East Lancs bodies styled by leading bus designer John Worker. At the time, East Lancs was closely associated with the British Bus group (it had been owned by predecessor Drawlane Transport from 1988) and this was expected to be one of the group's standard vehicles. The four-bay body has square-edged side windows and the top deck windscreen blends into a glazed area around the destination box. The driver's windscreen is barrel-shaped.

This was followed in 1997 by the Pyoneer (called Premyer until Plaxton objected to the similarity to its Première coach) fitted on other double-deck chassis. It has a double-curvature windscreen and lower dash also used on East Lancs' latest single-deckers. A lowfloor version was being developed in 1998, initially for the Dennis Trident.

BELOW: *East Lancs Cityzen: Before British Bus was acquired by Arriva, its Northumbria fleet bought some of the first Cityzens and put them on limited-stop services from Newcastle. Like all Cityzens, this one has a barrel-shaped driver's windscreen.*

BELOW: *East Lancs Pyoneer: The Pyoneer's double-curvature windscreen is the main difference from the Cityzen. This is a Capital Citybus Dennis Arrow operating in east London.* **Dennis**

ECW (see Leyland)

Leyland (including ECW, Park Royal, Roe)

A series of acquisitions and mergers led to Leyland owning Eastern Coach Works, Park Royal and Roe by 1965. It closed Park Royal in 1980, Roe in 1984 and ECW in 1987. Optare, which reopened the Roe works in 1985, built a few bodies under contract, but the ECW jigs were transferred to Leyland's Workington plant and production resumed there from 1988 until Volvo pulled out of British bodybuilding in 1991.

ECW
1966-81 standard

Built: Lowestoft, Suffolk
Height: High and low
Chassis: Bristol VRT, Leyland Fleetline, Atlantean
Main areas of operation: Throughout Britain, especially England

When Bristol developed the VRT, ECW simply adapted the basic design of five-bay body used on the front-engined Lodekka of 1960 for the new chassis and for the Atlantean and Fleetline. This has equal depth windows on both decks, narrow window pillars, separately mounted upper deck front windscreens and (on 9.5m chassis) a short upper deck side window above the engine. On highbridge bodies, the lower deck windows line up with the top of the driver's side window. Until 1972, all had flat windscreens; most built afterwards (including all VRTs) have BET-style double-curvature windscreens.

BELOW: *ECW: Highbridge version of the ECW body on a Go Ahead subsidiary's Leyland Atlantean, showing the higher position of the lower deck windows in relation to the cab and driver's windscreen. There also were 220 similar highbridge bodies fitted on VRTs, mostly for NBC fleets. Compare with the lowheight body illustrated on page 13.*

Park Royal/Roe 1968-81 standard

Built: Park Royal, London; Leeds
Height: High
Chassis: Leyland Fleetline, Atlantean
Main areas of operation: Manchester, Buckinghamshire, Birmingham, West Yorkshire, Nottingham

Park Royal and Roe developed a square profile four-bay body with equal depth windows on both decks and sides which taper in from the base of the upper windows. It was built on 9.5m and 10m chassis, the more common 9.5m having a short bay above the engine compartment. For a time, this was the standard body for London Transport, West and South Yorkshire, Greater Manchester and West Midlands PTEs and for some National Bus Company fleets.

Both bodybuilders made them with either curved or peaked front roof domes, but Roe fitted a more rounded peaked dome for the two Yorkshire PTEs. The standard driver's windscreen was vee-shaped with flat glass, but buses for NBC, Plymouth and Nottingham had Alexander-style two-piece curved windscreens and more elaborate lower front dash panels, while London Transport specified barrel-shaped windscreens. MCW also built similar bodies, but the Park Royal/Roe products can be distinguished by having single-piece front and rear roof domes and lower deck emergency doors that stop flush with the tops of the side windows.

BELOW: *Roe: A Southampton Citybus Atlantean, new to Plymouth, with the Roe version of the standard highbridge body. This has the Alexander-style windscreen and lower front dash first designed for London Country and chosen by some other operators.*

Olympian Body

Built: Leeds, West Yorkshire; Lowestoft, Suffolk; Workington, Cumbria
Height: High and low
Chassis: Leyland Olympian, Atlantean
Main areas of operation: Throughout Britain (notably London, Glasgow, Edinburgh, Newcastle, Liverpool, Manchester, Birmingham, Bristol, Preston, Isle of Wight, Blackpool, Leicester, Colchester, Southend, Reading, Cambridge, Norwich, Oxford)

Leyland developed the four-bay body for the Olympian from the Titan body, giving it shallower lower deck windows. On lowheight bodies, the windows on both decks are of equal depth. The rear upper deck emergency door on most has much more glazing than on the London Titans. Standard 9.5m models have equal length bays, but 10m bodies,

LEFT: ECW Olympian: A lowheight ECW-bodied Leyland Olympian in Stagecoach's United Counties fleet. This bus was built towards the end of the National Bus Company's existence and could well have been a much more common type had deregulation, privatisation and the end of Leyland not all happened between 1986 and 1991.

including one built on an Atlantean for Fishwick's of Leyland, have a shorter extra bay in the middle, as on RML Routemasters.

ECW and Roe built highbridge bodies with flat, vee-shaped two-piece driver's windscreens and with Alexander-shaped two-piece double-curvature screens; ECW built high and low models with BET windscreens. Optare built a few highbridge bodies under contract with vee-shaped and BET screens, while Workington built high and low models with BET screens. A key identification point is that Roe bodies and the first 15 Optare bodies (1985 models for West Yorkshire PTE and now operated by FirstGroup) have strapping over the panel joins on the sides.

ECW produced 52 coach bodies, mainly on 11m chassis, from 1982 to 1986. Most went to NBC subsidiaries for London commuter routes, but the survivors have long since been dispersed around the country. Most look like five-bay versions of the standard bus body with BET driver's windscreens, but have flat upper deck windscreens that rake back sharply; the last six and a 1984 prototype have more upright double-curvature upper deck windscreens and single-curvature driver's windscreens.

ABOVE: ECW Olympian coach: Forty-five of the Olympian coaches were fitted with this distinctive 11m version of the ECW bus body, with non-opening side windows and a raked, flat upper deck windscreen. This example, new to London Country, had migrated to Kelvin in Glasgow when photographed in 1998.

LEFT: Roe Olympian: A highbridge Roe-bodied Olympian, built for London Country with its specification of front end carried over from the Park Royal/Roe Atlantean body. It is in the blue and cream livery of Sovereign, the Blazefield company which inherited part of London Country North East, the last NBC subsidiary to be sold, and also operates former Stagecoach routes around Huntingdon in Cambridgeshire.

Marshall

Built: Cambridge
Height: High
Chassis: Leyland Olympian, Atlantean;
Dennis Dominator; Scania N112;
Volvo Ailsa, Citybus
Main areas of operation: Glasgow,
Derby, Leeds

Marshall only built double-deck bodies between 1978 and 1984. On this four-bay design, the top deck tapers in quite starkly from the base of the windows. Most have deeper lower deck windows. Upper deck windscreens are either two separate flat glasses or vee-shaped; they have vee-shaped flat driver's windscreens or BET screens.

BELOW: *Marshall: The last Marshall double-deckers were Volvo Citybuses for Derby. The undertaking renamed itself City Rider in the mid-1990s, but has since become Arriva Derby.*

Northern Counties Palatine I, II and predecessors

Built: Wigan, Greater Manchester
Height: High or low
Chassis: Leyland Olympian, Atlantean,
Fleetline, Lion; Dennis Dominator,
Falcon V, Arrow; Scania N112, N113;
Volvo Ailsa, Citybus, Olympian; DAF
DB250; MCW Metrobus
Main areas of operation: Manchester,
London, Liverpool, Glasgow, West and
South Yorkshire, Hull, Newcastle,
Teesside, Preston, Cambridge,
Norwich, Canterbury, Blackpool,
Preston, Nottingham

Northern Counties — owned by Plaxton since 1995 and in course of losing its identity — developed its four-bay body out of the needs of SELNEC (later Greater Manchester) PTE, an organisation that subsequently owned the company. It bears a strong superficial resemblance to contemporary Park Royal/Roe and MCW designs, but there are notable differences. It has thicker pillars to the sides of the upper deck front windscreens; a longer half-bay at the back of the upper deck of 9.5m models; a larger upper deck emergency door window; and most older models have ventilation louvres at the centre of the front roof dome. Some older vehicles have flat, vee-shaped driver's windscreens, but most have curved or barrel-shaped ones. Newer vehicles have recessed windows and separately-mounted upper deck front windscreens. Ten Mainline Dominators have Alexander R-type pillar spacing, driver's windscreens and lower front dash within the basic Northern Counties shape.

Until the mid-1980s, Northern

Counties supplied five- and six-bay bodies to Nottingham to its own peculiar, if practical, design. Front roof domes and upper deck windscreens on these buses are to East Lancs design, but rear domes on surviving models are similar to those on the four-bay body.

From 1988, the four-bay body gained peaked front roof domes, a restyled upper deck emergency door and a new lower front dash with a wide shallow grille. Pillar spacing on these and earlier bodies differs according to the length of the chassis. On 9.5m chassis, there is a small window between the entrance door and the front wheel and there is a thicker pillar after the first top deck side windows; longer vehicles lack these features, but on the later style of body, 9.8m Olympians have a short window immediately ahead of the engine compartment. The body was christened the Palatine in 1992 and three years later was

ABOVE: *Northern Counties: A Leyland Fleetline with Greater Manchester standard body (with that operator's three-section destination display) in service with Yorkshire Rider's Halifax division (now First Calderline) in 1994. Many similar Fleetlines and Atlanteans were sold in the mid-1980s when they became surplus to Manchester's needs.*

BELOW: *Northern Counties: One of 10 Mainline Dennis Dominators with unusual Northern Counties bodies. The front dome and upper deck windscreens are to the manufacturer's standard, but the rest of the body is very similar to the large numbers of Alexander RH bodies bought at the time — including the front grille.*

restyled with pointed-effect upper deck windows.

In 1993, the Palatine II body was added to the range, initially only on Olympian chassis but later on DAF and Dennis Arrow. This has deep single-curvature windscreens on both decks, deeper front side windows on the upper deck and a restyled lower dash; Olympians and DAFs have a front grille.

RIGHT TOP: *Northern Counties: A Capital Citybus Leyland Olympian with a later style of body with semi-peaked roof dome, thick rubber-mounted windows and curved windscreen. At the time, Capital Citybus was owned by a Hong Kong Chinese company, hence the characters incorporated into the fleetname and the '888' registration which is a lucky number in Chinese circles.* **Northern Counties**

RIGHT CENTRE: *Northern Counties Palatine I: The most recent and, probably, final version of the Palatine I lacks the peaked roof dome, but has the upper deck front windows raised in eyebrow fashion to a point. This is a lowheight 10m Volvo Olympian with Stagecoach Cambus.*

RIGHT BOTTOM:
Northern Counties Palatine II: A highbridge 10m Palatine II-bodied Volvo Olympian with First Glasgow.
Northern Counties

Optare Spectra

Built: Leeds, West Yorkshire
Height: High or low
Chassis: DAF DB250
Main areas of operation: Manchester, London, Poole, Southampton, Reading, Birmingham, Bristol, Eastbourne, Dundee

Although Optare bought the design rights to the MCW Metrobus body at the same time as DAF bought the chassis rights, it developed an entirely new body which went into production on the new chassis in 1991. This has deep windscreens on both decks and uses the Alusuisse bolted aluminium structure. It is available in low- and full-height versions and has been developed into lowfloor form with the launch of the DB250 in 1997. It has an unglazed lower deck rear end. Lowfloor models are available in two heights have longer top-deck side windows over the cab/entrance.

BELOW: Optare Spectra: A lowheight step-entrance Spectra on a DAF DB250 for Stevenson's of Uttoxeter, a company now absorbed into Arriva. Lowfloor versions have a long window above the front entrance and their top and bottom deck windows are out of alignment in the first bay. **Optare**

Park Royal/Roe
(see Leyland)

Plaxton President

Built: Wigan, Greater Manchester
Height: Low
Chassis: DAF DB250, Dennis Trident, Volvo
Main areas of operation: London, West Midlands.

Plaxton unveiled its prototype new generation lowfloor double-decker in October 1997 and anticipated putting it into production during 1998. The 2.55m-wide body is designed primarily for London with front end styling betraying a hint of East Lancs' Cityzen and Pyoneer.

LEFT: Plaxton President: The prototype two-door President body appeared at Coach & Bus '97 on a rear-engined Volvo concept chassis.

LEFT: Willowbrook: A Willowbrook-bodied Bristol VRT, new to East Kent when it was a National Bus Company fleet, in service with Arriva's sightseeing fleet in London.

LEFT: Willowbrook: The unique Baghdad-specification Atlantean operated by Whippet Coaches. The lower front dash is a Plaxton feature fitted when the bus was repaired.

Willowbrook

Built: Loughborough, Leicestershire
Height: High
Chassis: Bristol VRT, Leyland Atlantean, Dennis Dominator
Main areas of operation: London, Glasgow, Cambridgeshire

Willowbrook was a Duple subsidiary from 1958 until 1971 when it went its own way. Its occasional forays into the double-deck market included the supply of 117 bodies on Atlantean, VRT and Dominator chassis between 1977 and 1981 — mostly on VRTs for NBC fleets. This was similar to the Park Royal/Roe standard design, but had a more upright rear, BET windscreen and an ECW-influenced grille on VRTs.

An even rarer Willowbrook body still in service is on a 1980 Atlantean operated by Whippet Coaches in Cambridgeshire since 1987. This was one of a batch built for Baghdad to a Park Royal body design. It was damaged in shipment to Iraq and was repaired and converted to right-hand-drive. The six-bay body is unlike any Willowbrook or Park Royal body operated elsewhere in the UK. Subsequent rebuilding has given it some Plaxton coach parts.

Part 2. SINGLE-DECK BUSES

Chassis identification of single-deckers is more difficult than for double-deckers as bodybuilders are better able to disguise chassis features, especially on mid- and front-engined vehicles.

Chassis and Integrals — Rear- and Side-Engined

Blue Bird

Built: Fort Valley, Georgia, USA
1992 to date (for UK)
Engine: Cummins 6BTA
Transmission: Allison automatic
Bodywork: Blue Bird
Main areas of operation: South Wales, Hertfordshire, Staffordshire, West Sussex

Shipping costs have deterred American manufacturers from exporting many complete buses to Britain, but Blue Bird — one of the USA's largest school bus manufacturers — tried to establish a niche for itself with its relatively cheap heavy duty, high-floor, rear-engined vehicles with safety features that include hinged side windows which double as emergency exits. It hoped to sell them to operators looking for new

LEFT: Blue Bird: A Universitybus Blue Bird CSRE. These utilitarian buses have high floors and outward-hinged side windows which act as rapid emergency exits.

45

buses for school contracts. Shamrock Travel in South Wales has two Q-Bus models, a 31-seater and a 47-seater, while Universitybus in Hertfordshire and West Sussex and Staffordshire county councils between them bought 23 of the 12m CSRE model.

Bristol RE

Built: Bristol 1962-82
Engines: Gardner 6HLX, Leyland 680
Transmission: Self-Changing Gears semi-automatic
Bodywork: ECW, Alexander, East Lancs, Marshall
Main areas of operation: Northern Ireland, Warrington

The RE was the most successful of the first generation of rear-engined single-deckers produced from the mid-1960s. Leyland, which acquired partial control of Bristol in 1965, kept it in production longest for Ulsterbus and Citybus in Northern Ireland because they refused to buy the integral Leyland National, and could have the RE bodied by Alexander in Co Antrim. It was the standard single-decker for many National Bus Company fleets before the advent of the National. It has a horizontal engine and front radiator. Bus versions were the 10m RESL and 11m RELL; higher floor coaches were the 10m RESH, 11m RELH and 12m REMH. ECW bodies on 11m REs have six main window bays; 10m models have five. These are equal depth side windows with slim pillars. Models built between 1967 and 1970 had flat windscreens (taller from 1969); BET windscreens were fitted from 1970. Bus versions have a centrally mounted emergency door in the back, flanked by two tall windows; RELH semi-coaches have a large rear window and offside emergency door.

ABOVE: *Bristol RE: An ECW-bodied RELL with Hartlepool Transport. These and most other ECW-bodied REs have since been sold by their original owners, but several survive with secondary operators.*

DAF SB220

Built: Eindhoven, Netherlands 1988 to date
Engines: DAF 11.6-litre LC or 8.65-litre GS
Transmission: ZF automatic
Bodywork: Optare, Ikarus, Northern Counties, Plaxton, Alexander
Main areas of operation: London, Birmingham, Liverpool, Tyneside, West Yorkshire, Gatwick and Heathrow airports, North Wales, Teesside, Durham, Blackpool, Derby, Nottingham, Ipswich, York, Chester, Paisley

The 11.8m SB220, with horizontal rear engine and front radiator, went into production for the Dutch market in 1987 and was imported to Britain from October 1988, initially in an exclusive arrangement with Optare which developed its Delta body for the DAF chassis.

In 1990, Hughes DAF (now renamed Arriva Bus and Coach, DAF's UK importer and operator of a big bus and coach rental fleet) added the option of the steel-framed Ikarus 480 Citibus body built in the Hungarian capital, Budapest, by what used to be the world's largest volume supplier of buses and coaches. Ikarus has changed from building 12,000 vehicles a year for the former Soviet Bloc and world markets with which it traded, and now makes around 4,500 a year. The 480 is part of a range designed initially for North America and is only available in Britain on the SB220. Its most distinctive features are windscreen wiper mountings which cut into the lower dash panel and an extensive array of cooling grilles on the back panel. Hughes DAF also bought some SB220s with Northern Counties Paladin bodies.

The move to lower emission Euro 2 engines in October 1996 led DAF to redesign the SB220, fitting a nearside radiator and the smaller GS engine in place of the LC which is derived from (and sounds like) the Leyland 680. A more fundamental development was the 1997 UK launch of a lowfloor version of the SB220. It is available with Plaxton Prestige and Alexander ALX300 bodies and, hardly surprisingly in view of the group's importership, is the standard large single-decker for Arriva bus-operating subsidiaries.

The lowfloor SB220 is also available with a liquefied petroleum gas (LPG) engine — the only production bus on the UK market that works on this ultra-low-emission fuel. Plaxton-bodied examples have two long cylinders on their roof, one on each side. Early customers included First Crosville in Chester.

RIGHT: *DAF SB220: An Ikarus-bodied SB220 operated on a specially branded service for university students in Bath. The section of lower front dash from the windscreen to the bottom of the main headlamps hinges up for maintenance.*

Dennis Falcon H, HC

Built: Guildford, Surrey 1980-93
Engines: Gardner 6HLXB, 6HLXCT
Transmission: Voith, SCG, Maxwell
automatic
Bodywork: Duple, East Lancs,
Marshall, Wadham Stringer, Northern
Counties
Main areas of operation: Leicester,
Northampton, Grimsby, Ipswich,
Swindon, Merseyside, Greater
Manchester, Staffordshire

After selling 33 single-deck
Dominators, Dennis developed the
Falcon to fill the void left after Leyland
withdrew the RE from the market. The
Falcon H has a remote-located gearbox,
while the more common HC has the
gearbox coupled to the engine to create
a shorter rear overhang. Both models
sold mainly to municipal operators, but
Arriva has inherited some bought by
Drawlane and British Bus.

ABOVE: *Dennis Falcon HC: A Falcon HC, with East Lancs body, operated in Ipswich Buses'
rural fleet serving surrounding parts of Suffolk.*

Dennis Dart

Built: Guildford, Surrey 1988 to date
Engine: Cummins 6BT
Transmission: Allison automatic
Bodywork: Plaxton, Wright, Alexander,
Northern Counties, Carlyle, Duple,
Marshall, Wadham Stringer, UVG,
East Lancs
Main areas of operation: Throughout
Britain

The Dart has been by far the best
selling British bus throughout most of
the 1990s. It was developed as a
midibus and has grown larger, although

it is substantially lighter than many
vehicles considered full-size before. It
has a longitudinal engine and an offside
radiator. It was first built in three
lengths, 8.5m, 9m and 9.8m and has
leaf suspension. Air suspension became
standard with the introduction of the
slightly wider lowfloor Dart SLF (for
Super Low Floor) in 1995. The SLF
initially was offered in 9m, 10.2m and
10.6m lengths, although bodybuilders
tend to make them slightly longer. They
were followed in 1997 by the 11.3m
Super Pointer Dart, a semi-integral

variant with Plaxton body and Allison B300R gearbox in place of the AT545 unit in other Darts; an 8.5m version, the MPD (Mini Pointer Dart) was announced in 1998 as part of the SLF range.

The Dart is offered with a compressed natural gas (CNG) Cummins engine; examples of this ultra-low-emission Dart operate with FirstGroup fleets in Southampton and Bristol and can be identified by their roof-mounted tanks.

ABOVE: *Dennis Dart: Rear offside view of a step-entrance Dart operated by Stagecoach Cambus on park-&-ride services in Cambridge and fitted with Alexander Dash body.*

ABOVE: *Dennis Lance SLF: A Berkhof-bodied Lance SLF operated in Manchester by Stagecoach Ribble. Similar buses operate with Stagecoach East Kent and on BAA contracts at Heathrow.* **Dennis**

Dennis Lance

Built: Guildford, Surrey 1991-97
Engine: Cummins 6CTA
Transmission: ZF automatic
Bodywork: Plaxton, Wright, Alexander, Northern Counties, Wadham Stringer, East Lancs, Berkhof, Optare
Main areas of operation: London, Ipswich, Eastbourne, Bristol, Bath, Brighton, Tyneside, Birmingham, Merseyside, Dundee, West Yorkshire, Heathrow Airport, Bolton, Manchester, Canterbury, Southend, Harlow

Dennis continued the simple engineering philosophy which worked well on the Dart and developed the Lance as a 10.5m and 11.5m big brother. It has a larger, longitudinally mounted vertical engine, offside radiator in the engine compartment, air suspension and larger wheels. Whereas the Falcon has a ramped floor, the Lance's is flat to the rear axle. In 1993, Dennis led the market by developing the Lance SLF as the first British lowfloor bus and picked up an order for 38 from London Buses. The main customer for the original Lance was the Badgerline group (now part of FirstGroup) which bought it along with much larger quantities of Darts. The Lance has been a victim of the Dart's success and of its own shortcomings. It earned a reputation for being less reliable than the Dart and the development of the Dart SLF has offered a better combination of seating capacity and vehicle size to meet most Dennis customers' needs. The 10.5m version has only been built as the Arrow double-decker.

The most distinctive Lances are 40 SLFs — 10 with Stagecoach subsidiaries East Kent and Ribble, 30 with National Express subsidiary Speedlink at Heathrow — with Dutch-built Berkhof bodies. These steel-framed buses have bonded glazing and large barrel-shaped windscreens with quarterlights. Dennis turned to Berkhof when UK bodybuilders were unable to meet fast delivery dates for lowfloor single-deckers.

Iveco TurboCity

Built: Valle Uffita, Italy 1993
Engine: Iveco 8460.21
Transmission: ZF automatic
Bodywork: WS
Main areas of operation: South Wales, Lincolnshire, Coventry, Watford

Seven 12m TurboCity-U single-deckers were brought to Britain (see also double-deck section). An Alexander-bodied demonstrator was shipped to Malaysia and broken up, but the other six were bodied by WS Coachbuilders and sold to Shamrock of Pontypridd, Elsey's of Gosberton, Mike de Courcey of Coventry and Luckett's of Watford.

BELOW: *Iveco TurboCity: A Shamrock TurboCity with WS Coachbuilders Vanguard II body in service in Cardiff.*

Leyland National and B21

Built: Workington, Cumbria 1971-85, and (B21 for UK) Bristol 1980/4.
Engines: Leyland 510, 680, 690, TL11H; Gardner 6HLXB, 6HLXCT; Volvo THD100; DAF 11.6-litre; Cummins 6BT
Transmission: Leyland semi- and fully-automatic; ZF or Allison automatic
Bodywork: Leyland, Alexander
Main areas of operation: Throughout Britain, including London, Birmingham, Manchester, Liverpool, Glasgow, Sheffield, Lincoln, Reading, Sussex, Norfolk, Suffolk

ABOVE: Leyland National: A 10.3m Mk1 National, new to London Transport and operating with Universitybus in Hertfordshire.

More than 7,600 Leyland Nationals were built, making it the only mass-produced British bus constructed by the same methods as cars. It is an integral construction, highly standardised design produced in a purpose-built plant at Workington which has since closed. The model's name was chosen because it was produced in a joint venture with the National Bus Company which was by far its biggest customer. Nationals were also bought by all seven PTEs, London Transport, the Scottish Bus Group, many municipal undertakings, a handful of independents and major airports. Its highly durable body structure made it a popular secondhand purchase. The body shell also was used for some of the Pacer train fleet built for British Rail in the 1980s.

In their original form, Nationals have equal depth side and rear windows, a two-piece double-curvature windscreen and an angled roofline. Destination screens were to a common design, with provision for a display in a moulding above the large rear window.

Mk1 models, built until 1979 (there were 6,550 of these for UK and overseas customers), originally all had Leyland 510 engines, rear radiators and a grille on the back end. Until 1978, when the simpler Series B option was introduced, all Mk1 models had a heating pod at the rear of the roof (from 1976, this was made shorter); Series B models have floor-mounted heaters, no roof pod and a small grille between the headlamps. The National 2, which appeared in prototype form looking like a Series B, went into production in 1979 with the 680 engine in place of the ill-received 510, a front radiator and a more bulbous windscreen. Roof pods and plain roofs were available on this model which later was offered with Gardner engines and the quieter TL11H which ultimately ousted the 680.

Two lengths were built throughout the National's life. Mk1 models were either 10.3m or 11.3m, while National 2s were 10.6m or 11.6m to accommodate the front radiator. Long models have equal length windows in the main bays; short models have a longer bay immediately ahead of the rear axle, where a centre door can be fitted.

As they have got older, many Nationals — especially Mk1 models — have been repowered with Gardner, Leyland 680, Volvo and DAF engines and some have had their bodies refurbished. In 1991, East Lancs launched a refurbishment package called the National Greenway designed to add 10 years' life to ageing Nationals. This was partly to meet the needs of the Drawlane/British Bus companies which at that time were buying very few new buses, but was taken up by others — the most high profile of which was London General for its Red Arrow standee routes in central London. New fronts with a choice of barrel or flat vee-shaped windscreens and quarterlights, flat lower dash panels, curved rear ends derived from the EL2000 body, two-leaf doors, lower entrance steps and remounted side windows with square top corners are the most noticeable changes, which also involved a complete interior refit. Where replacement engines were fitted, these usually were Gardner or Volvo units.

British Bus later undertook a less expensive refurbishment programme, mainly on London & Country Nationals, to create a vehicle called the Urban Bus. This transplanted two of the most appreciated features of the Dennis Dart — the compact Cummins B-Series engine and Allison gearbox — into a National. Most of the original exterior features were retained, but two-leaf doors and shallower steps were fitted. A batch of these buses was rebuilt for London United in west London, but demand for refurbishment has fallen away and Nationals of all shapes and sizes are expected to disappear over the next few years.

Although Leyland did export several hundred Nationals, it encountered resistance from markets that insisted on buying chassis they could body locally. To overcome this, the semi-integral B21 underframe was launched in 1975, with some National running gear and a front radiator. Six of these Bristol-built vehicles, with Alexander (Belfast) bodies and a mix of Gardner and Leyland engines, went to Ulsterbus and Citybus in 1980 when RE production was coming to an end. Four 12m versions with Leyland 690 engines, cancelled by an Israeli customer, were bodied at Mallusk in 1984, fitted with Bristol badges and sold to Ipswich Buses which subsequently bought the Ulster vehicles. One of the Ulster B21s has since been sold on to Yorkshire Traction's Lincoln City Transport fleet.

ABOVE: *Leyland National 2: An 11.6m National 2, new to Trent and operating in 1998 for a long-established Derbyshire independent. Like the Mk1, this has the rear roof pod.*

Leyland Lynx

Built: Workington, Cumbria 1985-91
Engines: Leyland TL11H; Gardner 6HLXCT; Volvo THD102; Cummins L10
Transmission: Leyland or ZF automatic
Bodywork: Leyland, Alexander
Main areas of operation: Throughout Britain, including London, Birmingham, Bolton, Liverpool, Preston, Teesside, West Yorkshire, Bristol, Nottingham, Newcastle, Widnes, North and South Wales, Chester, Essex, Cardiff, Isle of Man

To replace the National, Leyland developed an 11.3m semi-integral underframe with a front radiator and a simpler driveline from its horizontal engine to the gearbox. The standard Workington-built body has flat sides, deep side windows with bonded glazing, squared-off wheel arches, an arched roofline similar to the National's, and flat windscreens — the driver's half of which is angled back in the fashion of British buses of the 1950s. Mk1 versions have flat fronts and a split-step entrance; Mk2 models, introduced in 1990, have a protruding grille and lower dash panel to accommodate intercoolers on Volvo-engined buses. Mk2 models also have a level entrance step. Six of the first Lynxes were supplied to Ulsterbus and Citybus in 1985 with Alexander (Belfast) bodies, but were sold to Stevenson's of Uttoxeter which now is part of Arriva Midlands North. They are the only British Lynxes not bodied by Leyland. Most Lynxes have Cummins L10 engines.

BELOW: Leyland Lynx: A first series Lynx with flat front and black grille in service with Universitybus. The Lynx 2 grille sticks out by an inch or so and is painted in the same colour as the main bodywork.

MAN 11.180, 11.190, 11.220, 14.220, 18.220, NL222

Built: Salzgitter, Germany 1991 to date
Engine: MAN D0826
Transmission: ZF automatic
Bodywork: Optare, Marshall, Alexander, East Lancs
Main areas of operation: Teesside, London, Reading, Derby, Glasgow, Motherwell, St Albans, Campbeltown, Heathrow Airport

MAN entered the British bus market in a joint venture with Optare, offering its Vecta body on the 10.1m 11.180 chassis which has a vertical engine and a nearside radiator in the engine compartment. This is a heavier duty equivalent of the Dennis Dart and has air suspension. The 6.9-litre engine developed 180hp. It took some time for it to establish a small niche in the market, but North East Bus (now part of Arriva), Trent, Reading and Hutchison's of Overtown all became loyal customers. The 11.180 was replaced by the 11.190 when Euro 1 emission standards took effect in 1993 and this, in turn, was replaced by the 11.220 for Euro 2 standards from 1996. By then, the relationship with Optare had ended and the 11.220 was bodied by Marshall; MTL London (since taken over by Metroline) and Dart of Paisley are two customers for this version. A lowfloor derivative, the Marshall-bodied 14.220, was due to be launched during 1998.

MAN has made a bigger breakthrough into the British market with the 18.220, a 12m lowfloor chassis with the same engine as the midibus. It won an initial order for 150, with Alexander ALX300 bodies, from Stagecoach during 1997. At the same time, it also imported an NL222 lowfloor chassis, with horizontal D0826 engine, and had it bodied by East Lancs for demonstration to potential customers.

BELOW: *MAN 11.180: An 11.180 with Optare Vecta body operated in Lanarkshire by Hutchison of Overtown.* **Optare**

Marshall Minibus

ABOVE: *Marshall Minibus: A pre-production Minibus operated on MTL London's Potters Bar town service. Larger versions of this body are fitted on Dennis Dart SLF and MAN chassis.*

Built: Cambridge 1995 to date

Engines: Cummins 4BT or Perkins Phaser

Transmission: Allison automatic

Bodywork: Marshall

Main areas of operation: London, Chester, Stockport

Although better known in the bus world as a bodybuilder, Marshall gained chassis manufacturing skills in 1992 by acquiring the remnants of the Bedford truck business. It used these combined resources to develop the 8.4m-long Minibus, a rear-engined lowfloor midibus with up to 27 seats and either a four-cylinder Cummins B-Series engine or Perkins Phaser. Both chassis and body use stainless steel to give a 25-year operating life. The body, with deep windscreen and winged 'M' badge, is a shortened version of the Capital body later developed for the Dennis Dart. When launched, the Minibus was smaller than the shortest Dennis Dart SLF and appeared to have filled a gap in the market as early orders for around 25 were secured from operators including London General, MTL London, Chester City Transport and Glossopdale, but teething troubles prevented it from building on these successes.

Mercedes-Benz O.405, O.405G, O.405N, OH.1416

Built: Mannheim, Germany 1992 to date

Engine: Mercedes-Benz OM447H, OM366A

Transmission: ZF, Voith or Allison automatic

Bodywork: Alexander, Wright, Optare, Mercedes

Main areas of operation: Birmingham, Aberdeen, Glasgow, Leicester, Teesside, Guildford, South Wales, Hull, Wolverhampton, Hertfordshire, Hereford and Carlisle

The 11.8m O.405 has been produced for the German and other markets since 1984 and has an OM.447H horizontal engine, offside radiator in the engine compartment and air suspension. The lowfloor O.405N had been introduced in Germany by 1990. When Mercedes brought the standard O.405 to Britain in 1992 and marketed it as the Cityranger, it had two chassis/windscreen structures fitted with Alexander PS bodies. Both subsequently became FirstGroup vehicles — a 51-seater for Midland Bluebird and an 18m, 60-seat articulated O.405G for First Aberdeen. A further 23, with 11.8m Wright bodies, went to those fleets and Stevenson's of Uttoxeter; these have Mercedes fronts married to Wright's Endurance design. In 1995, Mercedes teamed up with Optare to sell the O.405 as the Optare Prisma, with the Delta body (it has taller side windows than the Wright version) and Mercedes front. FirstGroup took 60 for fleets in Scotland and Leicester before turning away from Mercedes; other larger customers included North East Bus, Tillingbourne Bus, East Yorkshire and Rhondda Bus.

Mercedes adopted a different tack when it introduced the lowfloor O.405N in

BELOW: Mercedes-Benz O.405: A Wright-bodied O.405 Cityranger with gasket glazing and the shallow side windows that identify this bodybuilder's O.405s.

1997 and won an order for 100 from Travel West Midlands. Complete steel-framed buses were imported from Mannheim, with interior fitting and painting done in England. The first 11 were fitted out by UVG in Waterlooville, but work switched to Mercedes' own Wentworth Park preparation centre, near Barnsley, early in 1998.

In an earlier unsuccessful attempt to sell buses in Britain, Mercedes had just over a dozen OH.1416 chassis — an 11.5m model with OM.366A vertical engine, Allison gearbox and leaf suspension — bodied by Wright's with another version of its Endurance body, this time with 47 seats and the bodybuilder's own front end and marketed it as the Urbanranger. It was aimed at a virtually non-existent market for heavy duty interurban buses

and the biggest concentration of them went to Choice in Wolverhampton.

ABOVE: *Mercedes-Benz O.405: A Tillingbourne O.405 with Optare Prisma body operated on rural services in west Surrey. Note the taller side windows carried over from Optare's other designs.* **Optare**

BELOW: Mercedes-Benz O.405N: One of the first lowfloor integral O.405Ns for Britain in service in Birmingham with Travel West Midlands. The stepped side window line helps distinguish these vehicles.

Neoplan N416, N4009, N4014, N4015

Built: Stuttgart, Germany (for UK)
1987 to date
Engines: Gardner 6HLXCT, MAN
D0824, D2866, Cummins 6CTA
Transmission: ZF or Voith automatic
Bodywork: Neoplan
Main areas of operation: Essex,
Liverpool

Better known in the UK as the importer of exotic luxury coaches, Neoplan has also dabbled in the British bus market. Two N416 12m integral single-deckers were shipped to Britain in 1987 and put into the Sheffield-based SUT fleet then owned by the same people as Carlton PSV, the Neoplan importer. Their single-door bodies were built to the German VöV operators' SLII standard, but British taste was accommodated by having Gardner engines matched to their ZF gearboxes; Carlton assembled the second of the two in Yorkshire from a kit of German-supplied parts. Plans to import and sell another 13 were dropped and, following SUT's takeover by Mainline in 1989, the N416s were sold during 1996 to Nelson's of Wickford, in

BELOW: Neoplan N416: One of the two Gardner-engined Neoplans operated by Nelson's of Wickford. This one was assembled in Yorkshire; the other has a non-original front.

RIGHT: Neoplan N4009: One of the three 9m MAN-engined midibuses operated by MTL in Liverpool. Unlike most British vehicles built to this length, they are a full 2.5m wide, so they look particularly short and squat.

Essex. By then, one had been rebuilt with a Plaxton front dash and a DAB windscreen.

Neoplan's second assault on the market came in 1993/4 when British operators and PTEs became interested in lowfloor buses. Neoplan had been making lowfloor buses for 16 years by then. Merseytravel, the Merseyside PTE, ordered 15 German-style MAN-engined Neoplans for special MTL services in Liverpool. Twelve are N4014 12m models with D2866 engines and ZF gearboxes; three additional buses supplied in 1995 are 9m N4009 midibuses with D0824 engines and Voith gearboxes. By then, longer established suppliers were making lowfloor buses for the British market, but Neoplan hasn't given up hope and, in October 1997, unveiled a prototype right-hand-drive 12m N4015 based on a Cummins-engined, ZF-geared underframe made by Hungarian manufacturer Cspel.

Optare Excel

Built: Leeds 1995 to date
Engine: Cummins 6BT
Transmission: Allison automatic
Bodywork: Optare
Main areas of operation: London, Reading, Hull, Greater Manchester, Leicester, Nottingham, West Midlands, Blackpool, Ipswich, Motherwell.

When it launched its first lowfloor bus in October 1995, Optare characteristically did things differently from its competitors, producing a low-cost vehicle with midibus components but in dimensions that take it into the big bus category. The integral Excel uses the steel structure and Cummins B-Series engine of the MetroRider midibus described in Part 4 of this book. It is the first British bus fitted with the Allison B300R World Series gearbox. Unlike its then direct competitors from Dennis and Volvo, it is a full 2.5m wide; it is built in lengths of 9.3m, 10m, 10.7m and 11.4m. It has bonded glazing and is distinguished by its very large, barrel-shaped windscreen. Operators include Reading Buses, Travel West Midlands, East Yorkshire, Ipswich Buses, Blackpool Transport, Nottingham, First Leicester, Barton, Trent, Choice Travel and Hutchison's of Overtown.

BELOW: *Optare Excel: An 11.5m 39-seat Excel operated by Choice Travel of Wolverhampton.* **Optare**

Renault PR100

Built: Lyons, France (for UK) 1988/9
Engine: Renault MIPS 06.20.45
Transmission: ZF automatic
Bodywork: Northern Counties
Main areas of operation: Scunthorpe,
Luton airport

The PR100 French citybus was launched in the early 1970s by Berliet, a Citroën subsidiary acquired by Renault in 1975. The model was already on the verge of replacement when Renault entered into a joint venture with Northern Counties to build a steel-framed body between the Renault front and rear ends, a design distinguished by its flat, sloping windscreen and deep quarterlights. Only five were sold, three for airside duties at Luton airport and two which, after earlier careers (one with London Buses), operate with Hornsby of Scunthorpe.

BELOW: Renault PR100: One of the two PR100s operated by Hornsby. This one began life as a demonstrator.

Scania N113/N112, K92/K93/K112, L113, L94

Built: Katrineholm, Sweden 1980 to date
Engines: Scania DS9 (K92, K93), DS11 (N113, L113, K112), DSC9 (L94)
Transmission: ZF, Voith or Scania automatic
Bodywork: Alexander, Plaxton, Northern Counties, East Lancs, Wright, Van Hool.
Main areas of operation: London, Newport, Cardiff, Edinburgh, Glasgow, Dundee, Newcastle, West Yorkshire, Barnsley, Sheffield, Liverpool, Manchester, Chester, Shrewsbury, Luton, Hull, York, Ipswich; also Bristol and Heathrow airports.

Scania offered operators a choice of single-deckers during the 1980s and into the early 1990s, with single-deck versions of the N- and K-Series models described in the double-deck section. Transverse-engined N-Series single-deckers usually have the same bonnet assembly built into their bodywork as on the double-decker and share its offside radiator position between the axles and also have a nearside grille behind the rear axle. In 1993, a lowfloor version of the N113 was added to the range (30 with Wright bodies are operated by Arriva London North and

In August 1994, Scania broadened the appeal of its range by adding the L113 with a longitudinal engine which is inclined to take up less body space, and which is mated to a ZF gearbox in place of the N113's Voith. The L113's radiator is behind the rear axle on the offside. It is cheaper to buy and operate and is a British version of a model that has been available in Scandinavia and South America for some years. Initially, the L113 was offered only with step-entrance Alexander, Northern Counties and East Lancs bodies, but a lowfloor Wright's version — jointly marketed as the Axcess-ultralow — followed in 1995 and has become one of the standard 12m single-deckers bought by FirstGroup. The L94, a 9-litre successor to the L113 with a stronger chassis structure, was announced in 1997 and went into production the following year. A transverse-engined equivalent, the N94, is available in other markets.

ABOVE: Scania N113: Rear view of a First Midland Bluebird step-entrance N113 with Wright Endurance body incorporating bonded glazing and the registration number and route number display in the bottom of the back window — a layout that identifies Scania chassis under Wright bodies. Note the radiator grille ahead of the rear wheel and the side engine compartment door which also is fitted on double-deck N113s.

Stagecoach East London, 11 with East Lancs bodies run with First Leeds, Travel Dundee, Arriva Midlands North and Arriva Scotland West); unlike other lowfloor buses, these have an especially high rear section with three steps ahead of the rear axle.

BELOW: Scania L113: Note the more conventional offside rear radiator position on this Yorkshire Traction L113 with step-entrance Northern Counties Paladin body.

Spartan TX

Built: Charlotte, Michigan, USA
1995/6 (for UK)
Engine: Cummins 6BTA
Transmission: Allison automatic
Bodywork: East Lancs
Main area of operation: Barnsley

Even rarer than the Blue Bird, the American-built Spartan is a step-entrance 12m vehicle with similar drivetrain to the Dennis Dart. Yorkshire Traction operates the only two right-hand-drive examples imported into Britain; British Bus was also interested in the low-cost Spartan but was taken over by Cowie (now Arriva) before the project got under way.

LEFT: Spartan TX: One of Yorkshire Traction's two Spartans with East Lancs Opus 2 body. The most noticeable feature is the diamond-shaped Spartan badge on the front bumper. Delaine of Bourne has Volvos with similarly styled East Lancs Flyte bodies.
Bus & Coach Buyer

Van Hool A600, A308

Built: Lier, Belgium (for UK)
1989 to date
Engine: Cummins L10 (A600),
6BT (A308)
Transmission: ZF automatic
Bodywork: Van Hool
Main areas of operation: South Wales, Heathrow Airport

Like Neoplan, Van Hool is best known in Britain as a coach manufacturer, but it also builds integral buses for Belgian fleets, for several other European markets and North America. It looked seriously at Britain in 1989 when it brought over a 12m right-hand-drive A600 with a horizontal Cummins L10 engine, but the market collapsed then and the bus remained unique. It has since joined First Cymru in South Wales.

British Airways subsequently bought 28 lowfloor A308 midibuses for crew transport at Heathrow Airport. The Cummins B-Series engines in these 8.9m buses are mounted at the nearside between the two axles — a layout Van Hool pioneered to maximise floor space on lowfloor vehicles. The A600's side windows run up to roof level, but there is a load-bearing section above the windows on the A308s. Both models have sloping fronts with a large barrel-shaped windscreen.

ABOVE: *Van Hool A308: One of British Airways' side-engined lowfloor midibuses at Heathrow airport. The unglazed panel at the back conceals part of a walk-in luggage area reached by doors in the back of the bus. BA's ground transport fleet is now operated on its behalf by American transport giant Ryder.*

Volvo B6

Built: Vienna, Austria; Irvine, Ayrshire 1992 to date

Engine: Volvo TD63E, D6A

Transmission: ZF automatic

Bodywork: Alexander, Wright, Plaxton, East Lancs, Marshall

Main areas of operation: West Midlands, Greater Manchester, Glasgow, Perth, Dundee, Teesside, Sheffield, Lincoln, Blackburn, Gloucestershire, Cambridge, Heathrow Airport.

The Dennis Dart's runaway success prompted Volvo to develop a similar vehicle, using componentry from other buses and trucks in its range, and with air suspension as standard. It was known originally as the B6R and was intended to be a coach as well as a bus. The first were built by the Steyr Bus subsidiary in Vienna, which played a significant part in designing the vehicle, and six pre-production vehicles went to Stagecoach Cumberland along with a handful of others before the model was redesigned, relaunched as plain B6 and built in Scotland. The early Cumberland vehicles were sold after a couple of years. The B6 was offered in 8.5m, 9m and 9.9m lengths and, when badging is absent, the main distinguishing feature from the Dart is that its radiator is on the nearside of the engine compartment. In 1995, the 9.8m and 10.6m lowfloor B6LE was added. Neither the original B6 nor the B6LE has been anything like as popular as the Dart.

LEFT: *Volvo B6: Rear of a Mainline B6 with Plaxton Pointer body, showing the nearside grille. Window pillar spacing on B6 Pointers is wider than on equivalent Dennis Darts.*

RIGHT: *Volvo B10B: Rear of an MTL B10B with gasket-glazed Wright Endurance body. The B10B radiator is ahead of the offside rear wheel. Wright's fits rear registration numberplates and route number boxes in the tops of back windows on B10B, B10BLE and B10L models.*

Volvo B10B, B10BLE, B10L

Built: Borås, Sweden 1992 to date
Engines: Volvo THD103, 104; DH10A
Transmission: ZF or Voith automatic
Bodywork: Alexander, Wright, Plaxton, Northern Counties, Saffle
Main areas of operation: West Midlands, Greater Manchester, Liverpool, Glasgow, Edinburgh, Dundee, Tyneside, Teesside, Sheffield, West Yorkshire, Brighton, Oxford, Bristol, Northampton, Northern Ireland

The 12m B10B replaced the Leyland Lynx in Britain, but is used as the basis of a coach in some other markets like Spain and Israel. Its radiator is on the offside, ahead of the rear axle and the floor in the front section is lower than in the back. A lowfloor version, the B10BLE, was introduced in 1997 and has been ordered in quantity by FirstGroup, Go Ahead and Blazefield.

The B10BLE was Volvo's second lowfloor offering in this sector. In 1994, it launched the B10L which has a low floor along the full length of the bus. Its horizontal engine is set to the nearside — an unnecessary feature in Britain as it permits left-hand-drive models in mainland Europe to be fitted with a door and platform behind the rear axle. Its radiator is on the offside behind the rear axle. Most British B10Ls (for Travel West Midlands, Travel Dundee and FirstGroup's Manchester and Glasgow fleets) have Wright bodies, but Volvo offered it originally with a body designed by its own Swedish bodybuilding subsidiary, Saffle. A prototype was bodied in Sweden and the others were built by Alexander (Belfast) and called the Ultra. This has a fairly square profile with bonded glazing, either a single-piece or divided windscreen and a heavy load-bearing section above the windows. The Ultra body is designed to carry compressed natural gas (CNG) tanks on its roof and examples with this very low emission fuel are operated by Travel West Midlands in Walsall and by First Northampton. Diesel versions operate with Ulsterbus, Citybus, Timeline, First Glasgow, First Northampton and also with Dublin Bus.

A new rear-engined Volvo chassis, with a smaller engine, was expected to be launched by 1999 ready for Euro 3 emission standards coming in early in the 21st century.

ABOVE: Volvo B10L: A Timeline B10L with Swedish-designed Alexander Ultra body in service in Bolton. Note the radiator position, below the rearmost window. Newer Ultra bodies have divided windscreens, making them look even more like the Plaxton Prestige. Timeline was formed to take over leading coach operator Shearings' bus services in Shropshire and Greater Manchester.

Chassis and Integrals – Underfloor Mid-Engined

Underfloor mid-engined single-deckers became popular from around 1950 and, despite the move to rear engines from 1962, continued to be bought in substantial numbers as urban and interurban buses for another 35 years. In the 1970s, Bedford extended the concept to its lightweight range which was used mainly for rural, but also some urban routes. By the early 1980s, many bodybuilders were able to fit lower floors on to mid-engined chassis than had been the norm before, but the move to lowfloor buses with no steps in their entrance means that few are likely to be built in future. Stagecoach, which bought them for a wide range of routes including some of its big city services, bought its last Volvo B10M buses in 1998. Apart from the Leyland DAB, all mid-engined chassis listed in this section also have been built as coaches.

AEC Reliance

Built: Southall, Middlesex 1953-79
Engines: AEC AH470, AH505, AH590, AH691, AH760
Transmission: AEC semi-automatic and synchromesh; ZF synchromesh
Bodywork: Alexander, Duple, Marshall, Plaxton, Willowbrook

The Reliance was one of the longest-produced heavy duty underfloor-engined single-deckers on the market, graduating from a 30ft lightweight into a 12m vehicle more popular in its latter years as a coach. It ceased to be available after Leyland closed the AEC factory.

Bedford Y-Series, including Venturer

Built: Dunstable, Bedfordshire 1970-86

Engines: Bedford 466 (7.6-litre) and 500 (8.2-litre) diesel; Cummins 6BT and 6CT

Transmission: Spicer Turner, ZF synchromesh; Allison automatic

Bodywork: Alexander, Duple, Marshall, Plaxton, Wadham Stringer, Wright, Willowbrook

Bedford switched from front- to mid-engines in 1970, but whereas most other manufacturers fitted horizontal engines, Bedford retained a vertical unit, a layout that demands a higher floor and ground clearance. The Y-Series' model codes require some explanation: the 10m YRQ and 11m YRT had the 466 engine; their successors the YLQ and YMT had 500 engines (turbocharged in the YMT); the YMQ (later redesignated YMP) replaced the YLQ and also had a turbocharged 500; the 11m YNT and 12m YNV (also called the Venturer) had turbocharged 500 engines. Production of Bedford coach and bus chassis ended when General Motors pulled out of the truck and bus markets; as parts have become more difficult to obtain, some operators have had their Bedfords repowered with Cummins engines.

LEFT: *Bristol LH: A United Auto (now Arriva Durham County) LH with the wide version of the ECW body with which most — like this one — were built for the erstwhile National Bus Company. On narrow body versions, the trafficator lights are directly above the headlamps.*

Bristol LH

Built: Bristol 1967-81

Engines: Leyland 400, 401; Perkins H6/354

Transmission: Turner synchromesh; Self-Changing Gears semi-automatic

Bodywork: ECW, Alexander, Duple, East Lancs, Marshall, Plaxton, Wadham Stringer

The horizontal-engined LH was developed as a 9.2m lightweight single-decker for the National Bus Company's rural services. London Transport bought around 100 in the mid-1970s for routes that needed short, narrow buses. The 7.3m and 8.1m LHS remained in production longest; the 11m LHL coach was discontinued early in the model's history. Both LT and NBC bought LHs with ECW bodies superficially similar to those on Bristol REs; they have five bays, a large single rear window and, in most cases, BET-style windscreens (a few had flat windscreens). The London LHs, and some for NBC and others, had narrow bodies with trafficator lights above their headlamps; wide ECW bodies have trafficators outside the headlights.

Dennis Dorchester, Lancet

Built: Guildford, Surrey 1982-8

Engines: Gardner 6HLXB, 6HLXCT (Dorchester), Perkins 6.354 or V8; Leyland 402, 411, Cummins 6BT (Lancet)

Transmission: Voith automatic, Self-Changing Gears semi-automatic, ZF synchromesh (Dorchester); ZF synchromesh, Allison or Voith automatic (Lancet)

Bodywork: Alexander, Reeve Burgess, Wadham Stringer, Duple, East Lancs, Marshall

The heavy-duty Dorchester met a small level of demand for Gardner-engined single-deckers. Most common as a coach, bus versions survive with First Glasgow and Geoff Amos, a Northamptonshire operator.

The lightweight Lancet, available in 8m to 11m lengths, filled the gap left by Leyland's withdrawal of the LH. It has a vertical mid-engine with a relatively low step entrance to compensate for the otherwise high floor.

Dennis Javelin

Built: Guildford, Surrey 1987 to date

Engine: Cummins 6CTA

Transmission: ZF manual or automatic

Bodywork: Plaxton, Duple, Wadham Stringer

The 8.5m to 12m-long, medium-weight Javelin marked the start of Dennis's move from building niche market products to volume production. It is more popular as a coach than a bus, but bus versions were bought by Eastern Counties for rural services in Norfolk and Suffolk and by Eastbourne Buses. The Javelin's compact vertical engine and radiator are directly ahead of the rear axle to maximise luggage space between the axles.

Leyland Leopard

Built: Leyland, Lancashire 1959-82
Engines: Leyland O.600, 680; DAF
11.6-litre; Volvo THD100
Transmission: Leyland or ZF
synchromesh; Leyland semi or fully-
automatic.
Bodywork: Alexander, Duple, East
Lancs, Marshall, Northern Counties,
Plaxton, Willowbrook.

The Leopard was one of the most popular single-deck buses of the 1960s and 1970s, selling for years to the Scottish Bus Group, Ulsterbus and some smaller municipal fleets in South Wales and Lancashire. A few reconditioned chassis have been rebodied by Willowbrook, Plaxton and East Lancs; some have been repowered with DAF and Volvo engines. Originally a 30ft chassis, for most of its life the Leopard was built as the 10m PSU4, 11m PSU3 (the most common version) and 12m PSU5.

Leyland Tiger

Built: Leyland, Lancashire 1982-91
Engines: Leyland TL11H; Gardner
6HLXB, 6HLXCT; Cummins L10;
Volvo THD101
Transmission: Leyland semi-automatic;
ZF automatic or synchromesh
Bodywork: Alexander, Duple, East
Lancs, Plaxton, Reeve Burgess,
Wadham Stringer, Wright, ECW.

The Tiger replaced the Leopard. Its more powerful engines and air suspension helped counter competition from Volvo and other importers — the Gardner option was to compete with the Dennis Dorchester. Some bus chassis have leaf springs. Most were 11m or 12m long, but Tayside bought four special 9.5m models with Reeve Burgess bodies. The Cummins engine became standard towards the end after Leyland ceased making its own engines, but Ulsterbus/Citybus specified Volvo engines for its later deliveries; four Ulster-specification Tigers were delivered to Lowland (now part of FirstGroup) in 1991.

One even more unusual Tiger, included here for convenience rather than logic, is a solitary rear-engined model (a vertical TL11 mounted longitudinally) built in 1986 for demonstration in Bangkok and bodied by ECW to an equally unique design. It never reached Thailand, ran for a time with Leyland DAF's football club and then was sold to OK Motor Services in Co Durham — now part of Go Ahead.

RIGHT: *Leyland Tiger: The unique rear-engined Tiger built for Thailand but never shipped out of Britain and subsequently operated by OK. The ECW body was also unique.*

Leyland DAB

Built: Silkeborg, Denmark 1984/5

Engine: Leyland TL11H

Transmission: ZF automatic,
Leyland semi-automatic

Areas of operation: Sheffield, Leigh
(Greater Manchester)

Mainline has 13 DAB articulated 18m-long buses built in 1985 and now operated mainly on services between Sheffield city centre and the Meadowhall shopping centre. Their Danish bodies, built using the Alusuisse bolted system also adopted by Optare, Wright and East Lancs, have flat sides, Leyland National-style windscreens and large Continental-style destination screens.

In 1984, Leyland imported two similarly styled 9.9m DABs, badged as Tiger Cubs, to test demand for this size of vehicle. Both are now operated by Jim Stones in Greater Manchester. One has the same destination screen layout as the Mainline artics; the second (built for NBC and completed by ECW) has a taller windscreen with the destination fitted into the top. Both have single-leaf entrance doors.

BELOW: *Leyland DAB: One of the articulated DABs operated by Mainline on a busy cross-city route in Sheffield serving the Meadowhall shopping centre next to the M1. Until Stagecoach and FirstGroup revived interest in articulated coaches and buses, these were the only artics in regular service in Britain.*

Leyland Swift

Built: Leyland, Lancashire 1987-91
Engine: Cummins 6BT
Transmission: Turner synchromesh, Allison automatic
Bodywork: PMT, Reeve Burgess, Wadham Stringer, Wright

The 7.3m and 8.5m Swift was launched soon after Leyland Bus management bought the company from the Rover Group and it ended when Volvo axed every Leyland product except for the Olympian double-decker. The Swift's major units were from Leyland DAF's Roadrunner truck. The vertical engine is mounted behind the front axle and the radiator is directly in front of the engine.

Seddon Pennine 7

Built: Oldham, Lancashire 1973-82
Engine: Gardner 6HLXB
Transmission: Fuller synchromesh; Self-Changing Gears semi-automatic
Bodywork: (principal survivors) Alexander, Plaxton

Seddon, then an independent truck builder (following a series of takeovers, it's now part of Iveco), developed the Pennine 7 for the Scottish Bus Group as a Gardner-engined alternative to the Leyland Leopard. Over 500 were built, some as coaches, with a handful going to other fleets. Most were 11m long, although 12m models also were built.

Volvo B10M, B9M

Built: Borås, Sweden; Workington, Cumbria; Irvine, Ayrshire 1980 to date
Engines: Volvo THD100, 101, 102, 103; DH10A
Transmission: ZF synchromesh and automatic; Self-Changing Gears automatic; Allison automatic; Volvo synchromesh
Bodywork: Alexander, Duple, Caetano, Plaxton, Van Hool, Wadham Stringer, East Lancs, Northern Counties

The air-sprung, 12m-long B10M and its B9M 10m-long derivative — successors to the steel-sprung B58 sold in Britain from 1972 — are sold mainly as coaches. The B10M is the best-selling single-deck chassis in Britain and also is the best-selling mid-engined chassis in Europe. Bus versions (some are 11m long) have been bought by several operators, most notably Stagecoach, but other customers include Ulsterbus, Mainline, Travel West Midlands, Trent, Timeline, Badgerline, Blackburn and First Glasgow. The B10M was built at Workington in 1990/1 and at Irvine from 1995. The fourth series of B10M, launched in 1993, has a nearside radiator directly behind the front axle.

In the 1980s, Volvo imported three lighter single-deckers, two front-engined B57s and a mid-engined B7M.

ABOVE: *Volvo B10M: Among the more unusual B10Ms are four with Portuguese-built Caetano Stagecoach bodies built in 1985. The body name has no connection with what is now one of Britain's biggest bus operators. It was developed when manufacturers thought that coach operators would run deregulated bus routes with dual-purpose single-deckers. All four ended up with big groups: this is one of three with what now is First Glasgow; the other is with Arriva's London & Country fleet. Two of the Glasgow buses have gasket-glazed windows; this one and the Arriva vehicle have bonded glazing. The basic body style is to the German VöV pattern built mainly by Mercedes, Neoplan and MAN.*

Chassis - Front-Engined

In the years before larger truck-derived minibuses became common, lightweight front-engined chassis were bought for rural services. These used many components from their manufacturers' truck ranges and were even more popular as coach chassis. During the 1970s, some of these models also were bought for interurban and urban routes. They are fast disappearing.

Bedford SB/NJM, VAS/PJK

Built: Dunstable, Bedfordshire 1950-86
Engines: Bedford diesel and petrol; Leyland diesel; Perkins diesel
Transmission: Synchromesh
Bodywork: Willowbrook, Marshall, Reeve Burgess, Wadham Stringer, Wright

The 40-seat SB (known as the NJM towards the end of its life) was Britain's longest-produced bus chassis, spanning the period from the end of the postwar travel boom to Bedford's demise as a volume truck and bus builder. It has a front engine, mounted over the front axle, next to the driver, with the entrance normally immediately behind the front axle. The smaller VAS (known latterly as the PJK) was first built in 1961 and was a midibus before the term was coined. It takes bodies seating around 30.

Ford R-Series

Built: Langley, Buckinghamshire 1963-85

Engine: Ford diesel or petrol

Transmission: Synchromesh; Allison automatic

Bodywork: Alexander, Duple, ECW, Marshall, Plaxton, Wadham Stringer, Willowbrook

Ford's 10m and 11m single-deckers first appeared in 1963 as the Thames Trader 676E, but became the R-Series two years later. Until 1977, they had a vertical engine ahead of the front axle, between the driver and the entrance door; for the remaining eight years of production, the engine was inclined to sit below floor level, with the floor ramped up to the front. Between 1965 and 1971, 10m models were R192 and 11m models were R226 (192 and 226in wheelbases); they became R1014 and R1114 (10m or 11m, 140hp) in 1971 and R1015 and R1115 in 1982 when a 150hp engine was fitted. The National Bus Company, one of its bigger customers in the 1970s, had a few cut down to midibuses; Ford later offered a Tricentrol midi conversion, the T152.

Leyland Cub

Built: Bathgate, West Lothian 1979-86

Engine: Leyland 6/98

Transmission: Turner synchromesh; Allison automatic

Bodywork: Duple, HTI-Maxeta, Optare, Reeve Burgess, Wadham Stringer

The Cub was a midibus version of Leyland's Terrier truck and sold more into the welfare/school bus market than as a service bus. It has a vertical engine mounted either ahead of the front axle (when the axle is set back behind the entrance) or directly above it.

BODYWORK

Most single-deck bodies are quite clearly either buses or coaches, but a few have been built as both. For the sake of simplicity, some coaches (eg Alexander TC) are shown under the bus heading because they were developed from a bus, while others (eg Duple Dominant E, Van Hool Alizée and Jonckheere bus) are derived from coaches and are described in the coach section.

Alexander Y-type

Built: Falkirk, Stirlingshire; Mallusk, Co Antrim

Chassis: Leyland Leopard; Seddon Pennine 7; Bristol RE; Bedford Y-Series; Ford R-Series; Dennis Lancet; Volvo B57; AEC Reliance

Main areas of operation: (principal survivors) Scotland, Northampton, Leicester

The first Y-types appeared in 1961, the last (on a Lancet and a B57) in 1982. For most of that period, it was the Scottish Bus Group's standard single-decker (SBG bought over 2,800 on front-, mid- and rear-engined chassis) and it sold to several other UK operators. A few were built by Alexander's Ulster subsidiary and its predecessor, Potter of Belfast. Y-types were built from 9.5m to 12m lengths with interior finishes ranging from basic service bus to luxury coach.

All have the same design of double-curvature front windscreen, widening from top to bottom (both single-piece and divided), and the same two-piece rear window which narrows from top to bottom. Glass fibre front grille designs have changed over the years; Bristols, with front radiators, had larger grilles. The long window version, more often a semi-coach than a bus, has three main window bays (four on the very few 12m examples), all with gently forward-sloping pillars. The short window version, usually a bus, has upright window pillars and twice the number of window bays.

LEFT: *Alexander Y-type: A Clydeside (now Arriva Scotland West) Leyland Leopard with a bus-seated version of the long-window AY body (the 'A' is for 'alloy').*

LEFT: *Alexander Y-type: Rear view of a First Midland Bluebird Leopard with the short-window AYS body. This one has a rear luggage boot.*

Alexander T-type

Built: Falkirk, Stirlingshire

Chassis: Leyland Leopard, Tiger; Seddon Pennine 7; Dennis Dorchester

Main areas of operation: (principal survivors) Scotland, Northern Ireland

To complement the Y-type with a body better suited to coach work, Alexander created the higher-floored T-type in 1974 and began volume production two years later. The body tapers in from the base of the windows, has taller side windows than the Y-type and a flatter roof profile. As built before 1983, it has identical windscreen and rear windows — two-piece curved, narrowing from the bottom and, at the front, stopping in line with the top of the passenger door — with a destination box set above it. These vehicles have a grille design derived from the Y-type.

In 1983, the T-type was facelifted with a taller windscreen incorporating a destination display behind the top of the glass, a less elaborate grille confined to the bottom of the front dash and a shallow single-piece rear window. Some older Scottish Bus Group T-types also were retrofitted with shallower rear windows. There are three versions of the later T-type: the dual-purpose/express service TE; the service bus TS with opening side windows and fewer body mouldings; and the TC coach with a different grille and plug-type single-piece door. Some TCs have bonded glazing or square-edged gasket glazing, but others have round-edged windows. Some TEs are operated by Bus Eireann in the Irish Republic.

LEFT: Alexander TS: A TS body, on Gardner-engined Leyland Tiger chassis, with Kelvin. Behind it is a lowheight Alexander Royale-bodied Volvo Olympian.

BELOW:

Alexander T-type: An example of the original design of T-type body on a Fife Scottish (Stagecoach) Leyland Leopard in Dundee. This was one of the last Leopards supplied to the Scottish Bus Group in the early 1980s.

Alexander
P/PS-type

Built: Falkirk, Stirlingshire
Chassis: Leyland Tiger; Volvo B10M;
Scania K92, K93, N113; Mercedes-Benz
O405; Dennis Lance, Lancet
Main areas of operation: Aberdeen, Fife,
Glasgow, Dundee, Newcastle, Cumbria,
Lancashire, Greater Manchester, Hull,
South Yorkshire, Derby, Nottingham,
Sussex

The 11m and 12m P-type was
launched in 1983 to replace the Y-
type. In its original form, it has
very flat sides, sharply angled front
corner panels, flat windscreens
(single-piece and divided) and
quarter-lights. The nearside front
corner has either a second
quarterlight or else has a deeper,
extended quarterlight for kerbside
visibility. The tall side windows are
of a similar short length to the Y-
type bus. The stark styling was
partly because Alexander hoped to sell
P-type kits for assembly overseas. Its launch
coincided with a drop in demand for large
single-deckers at home and sales were
relatively limited, mainly to a few Scottish
Bus Group fleets, East Midland,
Badgerline, West Midlands Travel, Burnley
& Pendle and Grimsby Cleethorpes on
Tiger, Lancet and B10M chassis.

The P-type's fortunes were changed in
1988 when it was restyled
for Singapore and
relaunched as the PS (the 'S'
was for Singapore). It was
given a new front end with a
double-curvature windscreen
incorporating a destination
display, while the back end
was also tidied up. The first
PS bodies for the UK were
on Scania chassis; some early

Dennis Lances got this body and the
first two Mercedes-Benz O405s for
Britain have PS bodies with Mercedes
front ends. But by far the most
common chassis is the B10M.
Stagecoach alone has over 500, while
Mainline has 180 in South Yorkshire,
and Kelvin bought nearly 200 for
services around Glasgow before it was
taken over by FirstGroup. Production
ended in 1998.

ABOVE: *Alexander P: An early P-type on
a Perkins-engined Dennis Lancet chassis in
service with Redby in Sunderland. The bus
was new to Northen Scottish.*

BELOW: *Alexander PS: One of
Stagecoach's large fleet of Volvo B10Ms
with PS bodies. This is in the special red
and cream park-&-ride livery used in
Cambridge.*

Alexander Belfast bodies, including N-type and Q-type

Built: Mallusk, Co Antrim
Chassis: Leyland Leopard, Tiger, Lynx, B21; Bristol RE, LH; Bedford Y-Series; Ford R1015; Volvo B10M
Main areas of operation: Northern Ireland, Ipswich, Lincoln, Greater Manchester, West Midlands, Staffordshire/Cheshire, Darlington, Scottish Borders, Derby

In 1968, Potters of Belfast — the predecessor of Alexander's Belfast subsidiary — started to build a standard body for Ulsterbus single-deckers. When built at the Falkirk factory on some Bristol RELLs, it was called the PU-type (probably for 'Potters Ulsterbus'), but it appears to have had no code at Mallusk. Its sides, with window bays halfway in length between the extremes of the Y-type bus and semi-coach, are closely akin to Willowbrook bus bodies of the day, even down to some of the side mouldings and angled rear window. The front has a standard Alexander windscreen, but with a plainer front dash and, usually, a substantial bumper. Bristol RELLs have a central emergency exit at the rear and a large front grille. This style of body went on the Leyland B21s built for Ulsterbus and its Citybus sister fleet in Belfast.

In 1984, this design was superseded by the more aerodynamic N-type which also was built on some Ford school buses. It has a more angular outline with a P-type flat windscreen and a square grille. Although built mainly on Tigers, the N-type also went on Ipswich's B21s and Ulsterbus's Lynxes. Shearings bought N-type Tigers for its short-lived bus operations and when Timeline, the company that took over this arm of the business, sold them, several were bought by Midland Red North, now part of Arriva.

In 1990, the N-type gave way to the Q-type, the last model designed and built exclusively at the Northern

ABOVE: *Alexander Belfast: An ex-Ulsterbus/Citybus Leyland B21, with Mallusk-built body, in service in Ipswich.*

RIGHT: *Alexander N-type: One of Ipswich's 12m B21s with the N-type body.*

Ireland factory. It has a more rounded front, introducing the design feature of a windscreen that curves deeply at the bottom. Apart from the Ulster fleets and Shearings, United Auto (now Arriva North East), Lowland (now part of FirstGroup) and Trent all bought Q-types. Production ended in 1994.

ABOVE: *Alexander Q-type: A Timeline Volvo B10M with Q-type body in Warrington bus station. The windows are cleverly shaped so the flat glass appears to be curved.*

Alexander Dash, Strider

Built: Falkirk, Stirlingshire
Chassis: Volvo B6; Dennis Dart (Dash); Volvo B10B; Scania N113, L113; Dennis Lance (Strider)
Main areas of operation: Aberdeen, Edinburgh, Glasgow, Newcastle, Lake District, West Yorkshire, Harrogate, York, Greater Manchester, South Yorkshire, Nottingham, West Midlands, Gloucester, Southampton, Sussex, East London, Cambridge, Norwich, Cardiff, Newport

Alexander turned briefly from codes to model names as it introduced new bodies for rear-engined chassis, starting in 1991 with the Dash midi body which was followed in 1993 by the similar looking 12m Strider (the name was a play on Yorkshire Rider, the model's first customer). Both have a similarly square profile with a deeper roof coving than the PS, a separate destination box above the divided, double-curvature windscreen and a cab window that slopes down to meet the bottom of the windscreen.

When it was launched, the bottom of the Dash's windscreen deepened to a point, and it had a recessed ventilation duct between the headlamps, but from early 1995 it was restyled with a similar flat-bottomed windscreen to the Strider and gained a 'smiling' mock grille with Scottish Saltire logo in place of the recessed duct. The Strider has a plain lower dash. Most models have round-edged glazing, but West Riding/Yorkshire Buses (now Arriva Yorkshire) bought them with square-edged double glazing. Large Dash fleets are operated by Stagecoach.

BELOW: *Alexander Dash: The original Dash, with plain lower dash and a pointed base to the windscreen, on a Stagecoach United Counties Volvo B6.*

BELOW: *Alexander Dash: The later design of Dash, with straight-bottomed windscreen and Saltire mock grille. This is operated by Oban & District on former Midland Bluebird routes in Argyllshire.* **Alexander**

ABOVE: Alexander Strider: The Strider sold to both of the larger South Wales municipal bus companies, both of them taking it on Scania chassis. This is a Cardiff Bus N113; Newport has N113s and L113s. **Alexander**

Alexander
ALX200, ALX300

Built: Falkirk, Stirlingshire
Chassis: Volvo B6LE; Dennis Dart
SLF (ALX200); Volvo B10BLE, DAF
SB220, MAN 18.220 (ALX300)
Main areas of operation: Glasgow,
Perth, East Lothian, Tyne and Wear,
Derby, West Yorkshire, London,
Manchester, West Midlands,
Gloucestershire, Devon, Cambridge,
Oxford, Winchester

Following the Mayflower Corporation's acquisition of Alexander in August 1995, a completely new range of mainly lowfloor bodies was commissioned from prolific freelance designer John Worker. The 2.4m-wide ALX200 midi appeared in November 1996 and was followed 11 months later by the 2.55m-wide ALX300 on 12m chassis. Both have vertically divided double-curvature windscreens, but a clever design trick gives them a black moulding to create the effect of a deeper curved bottom

RIGHT Alexander ALX200: One of the first of 90 Volvo B6LEs with gasket-glazed ALX200 bodies for Stagecoach which also has the same body on Dennis Dart SLFs. This is operated in Perth, headquarters of the international transport group. **Alexander**

79

BELOW: *Alexander ALX300: The first of what is expected to be a large fleet of ALX300-bodied DAF SB220s for Arriva fleets. It has bonded glazing and is in the group's blue and sandstone corporate colours. Note the nearside grille which helps identify the DAF chassis. Compared with the 2.4m-wide ALX200, this body is higher and one of the few visual clues to the extra width is in the angle of the windscreen wipers.*
Arriva Bus & Coach

reminiscent of the Q-type windscreen. They have round head and tail lamps, a square profile with deep coving, and square-edged windows, bonded on the ALX300. Stagecoach and Arriva were the main early customers for both models.

Carlyle (and Duple and Marshall) Dartline

Built: Blackpool, Lancashire; Edgbaston, Birmingham; Cambridge
Chassis: Dennis Dart
Main areas of operation: London, Southampton, Durham, Hereford, Hertford, Shrewsbury, Epsom, Rochdale, Ramsgate, Great Yarmouth, North Hertfordshire, Greater Manchester

When the Dennis Dart was first developed in 1988, Dennis and Duple were both owned by Hestair, so it made sense for it to be offered exclusively with a Duple body known as the Dartline. The distinctive design — with bonded glazing, an S-shaped front with an asymmetric barrel-shaped windscreen which was slightly deeper on the nearside — used the Cromweld stainless steel structure Duple had pioneered on its 425 coach. By the time the Dart went into production in 1989, Hestair had sold its vehicle-building interests to its management which, in turn,

had sold the rights to most of the Duple body designs to Plaxton. The Dartline body would have gone, too, had Plaxton wanted it, but it developed its own Pointer body instead. Carlyle, a privatised minibus builder formed out of National Bus Company subsidiary Midland Red's engineering works in Edgbaston, bought it and took over production in the winter of 1989/90 soon after the first vehicles were built in Blackpool. Rival bodies soon outsold the Dartline and Carlyle went into liquidation in 1991, with its bus bodying business going to Marshall's the following year. Before redesigning the body, Marshall completed five Dartlines — two for Mayne's of Manchester (since sold on to Rossendale Transport) and one each for Epsom Buses, Williamson of Shrewsbury and Myall's of Bassingbourn. On most 8.5m and 9m models, the destination box is built into the top of the windscreen; 9.8m versions have a taller box above the windscreen. The 8.5m and 9.8m Dartlines have a shorter window bay in the middle, the 9.8m version having three main windows in the front half.

Duple Dominant

Built: Blackpool, Lancashire
Chassis: Bedford Y-Series; Bristol LH; Dennis Lancet, Falcon H; Ford R-Series; Leyland Cub, Leopard, Tiger; AEC Reliance; Volvo B10M
Main areas of operation: Swindon, South Wales, Greater Manchester, Cambridge, Luton, Essex

The Dominant bus, built from 1974 to 1987, uses the same pillar spacing as the Dominant coach launched in 1972 and has the same headlamp and grille arrangement as the original coach design. The arched roof profile, deep destination display area and curved two-piece windscreen were influenced by the Leyland National. The deep side windows are of equal depth on the vast majority of Dominant buses, but Falcon Hs in the Thamesdown fleet at Swindon and a handful of B10Ms have deeper windows in the two frontmost bays to increase visibility for passengers in vehicles with lower floors towards the front.

BELOW: *Duple Dominant: A Bedford YMQ with Duple Dominant bus body, new to South Wales Transport in NBC days. It was photographed operating in Cambridge with Whippet Coaches.*

Duple 300

Built: Blackpool, Lancashire

Chassis: Dennis Javelin; Leyland Tiger; Volvo B10M

Main areas of operation: Co Durham, Norfolk, Suffolk, Essex, Greater Manchester, Northampton, Ayrshire, Lanarkshire

The successor to the Dominant bus, built from 1987 to the end of coach production at Blackpool in 1989, also is based on a coach structure. The 300 is built on a 3m-high version of the 320 coach structure and has its roof profile and lower front dash. It has a wide entrance door and square-edged gasket glazing. First Eastern Counties operates Dennis Javelins with the 300 body; larger fleets operating Volvo B10M-chassised 300s include First Northampton and Stagecoach A1 Service in Ayrshire.

BELOW: *Duple 300: A Leyland Tiger with Duple 300 body new to short-lived operator Jubilee of Stevenage and operating in Harlow new town with County Bus, now Arriva East Herts & Essex.*

East Lancs EL2000 and predecessors

Built: Blackburn, Lancashire

Chassis: Dennis Dominator, Falcon, Lancet, Lance, Dart; Leyland Tiger, Leopard, Atlantean; Volvo B10M, B58, B7M, B6; Bristol RE, LHS; Scania K92, K93, K112, N112

Main areas of operation: London, Greater Manchester, East Lancashire, Hull, Grimsby, Hartlepool, Ipswich, West Yorkshire, South Wales, Glasgow, Tayside, Lincolnshire, Staffordshire, Merseyside, Leicester, Surrey

For the best part of 30 years from the mid-1960s, East Lancs' single-deckers were characterised by the same bespoke building approach that created so many variations in its double-deck designs. The basic original body had flat sides, long side windows and a very large

sloping rear window to aid drivers when reversing. Windscreens originally were Alexander-style double-curvature units and roofs were rounded, but flat two-piece screens and tapered-in roofs above the window line became features in later years.

In 1986, a bow-sided design was launched, initially on Scanias, but later also on Tigers. Its flat side windows are set high in the body and windscreens either are flat, deep curved or shallower Alexander-style double-curvature.

In 1990, this design evolved into the aluminium-framed EL2000, also with bow sides. It has deeper side windows and a rounded back with a high-set rear window very similar to Van Hool's T8 coaches. Within the EL2000's basic structure, there were many opportunities for design variations, especially with the same windscreen choice as before; some Arriva companies have B10Ms rebodied for the Grey Green fleet and fitted with shallower Alexander R-type side windows. The EL2000 has been used to rebody other older chassis, including some Atlanteans converted from double-deck and, in some instances, lengthened. A shorter and narrower version has been built on Dart and B6 chassis.

BELOW: *East Lancs EL2000: A Leyland Atlantean rebodied for Southampton Citybus as a single-decker with an EL2000 body.*

East Lancs MaxCi, European

Built: Blackburn, Lancashire
Chassis: Scania N113 CRL, L113
Main areas of operation: Glasgow, Dundee, Shrewsbury, Luton, Leeds, Newcastle, Barnsley

The close working relationship between East Lancs and Scania — forged when the N113 double-decker was brought to Britain and which later saw single- and double-deck bodies developed for the K-Series — came into play in 1993 with the launch of the N113 CRL MaxCi, Scania's first generation lowfloor model. Scania was already building complete left-hand-drive models for the Scandinavian market with its own stainless steel-framed bodies, so East Lancs was commissioned to build the same body for Britain. It has a very square profile, with a shallow double-curvature divided windscreen, bonded glazing and an unusual window arrangement with the side glazing sweeping up sharply to follow

BELOW: East Lancs MaxCi: One of the rare Scania MaxCi lowfloors operating with Arriva Scotland West. Note the raised window line in the rear section.

BOTTOM: East Lancs European: Arriva The Shires operates Scania L113 chassis with the step-entrance Swedish-designed body built by East Lancs and fitted with a more conventional window line.

the raised rear section; because most of the side windows are of equal depth, the tops of the rear section windows are higher than those of the front section. It also has a very high back window.

Only 11 MaxCi models were built and nine were sold to British Bus which then was closely related to East Lancs. It had a little more success with the similar-looking European body on the L113. This has the same square profile, shallow windows and windscreen as the MaxCi, but isn't a lowfloor vehicle and all its side windows start and finish at the same level. Sixty-four were built in 1994/5, five for Yorkshire Traction and the others for British Bus fleets Clydeside, Northumbria, Midland Fox and The Shires (all now part of Arriva).

East Lancs Spryte, Flyte and Opus 2

Built: Blackburn, Lancashire
Chassis: Scania L113, K112;
Dennis Dart; Volvo B6, B10M;
MAN NL222; Spartan TX
Main areas of operation: Glasgow,
Dundee, Luton, Barnsley, Sheffield,
Peterborough, Liverpool, East
Lancashire, Surrey

In 1995, East Lancs began transforming its range by phasing in Alusuisse bolted aluminium construction and commissioning John Worker to design some eye-catching new products. The first Alusuisse bodies, on Yorkshire Traction's Spartan TXs, were called Opus 2. This model, with flat canted-in sides, gasket glazing, a deep coving section above the side windows, and the EL2000's double-curvature windscreens, was a prelude to Worker's new Spryte and Flyte, launched in 1996.

The Spryte, on Dart and B6 chassis, is the midi body; the Flyte is the 12m version.

Both have gasket glazing, a deep double-curvature windscreen, a separate destination box that projects above roof level, a raised lip-effect moulding between the headlamps, a large rear window and round tail lamps. A Nottingham B6 has been rebodied with a narrow step-entrance Spryte body, and Yorkshire Traction has had Scania K112s fitted with new Flyte bodies. Lowfloor models have deeper side windows. Although most have been built to the standard specification, Delaine of Bourne has two Flyte-bodied B10Ms with EL2000/Opus 2 windscreens.

BELOW: *East Lancs Spryte: A Dennis Dart SLF in service in Liverpool and fitted with the John Worker-designed Spryte body. Spryte and Flyte bodies on step-entrance chassis have shallower side windows.*
Dennis

Marshall

Built: Cambridge

Chassis: Dennis Dart; Volvo B6; MAN 11.220

Main areas of operation: London, Cambridge, Liverpool, Widnes, Greater Manchester, Newcastle, Oxford, Brighton, Cardiff, Exeter, Glasgow, Dundee, Luton, Barnsley, Sheffield, Peterborough, Liverpool, East Lancashire, Surrey, Isle of Man

Marshall has had two phases of bus bodybuilding. In 1959, it bought Birmingham-based Mulliner's bus-making interests and transferred them to its Cambridge airport works; that lasted until 1985 and included a mix of home market and export sales of civilian and military buses. In 1992, it bought the Carlyle business out of liquidation, also transferring it from Birmingham.

After buying the Carlyle business, Marshall redesigned the Dartline body to overcome some perceived weaknesses and relaunched it in 1993 on the Volvo B6 as well as the Dart. The main changes were to give it gasket glazing, with the side windows stepped up in the rear section, restyled domes, equal depth windscreens and a revised lower front moulding to protect the windscreen from slow speed accident damage as, before, it stuck out farther than the front bumper. This body, which was given various names and codes by Marshall which never stuck, was first built on 14 unusual 8.5m B6s for Cambridge-based Cambus (now part of Stagecoach), but most have been on Darts — notably for Go Ahead fleets. Metroline has this style of body on MAN 11.220s.

In 1995, this was replaced by a larger version of the body fitted on the Marshall Minibus, with deep double-curvature windscreens, a sloping back window and equal depth side windows in the main bays. On lowfloor Dart SLFs, it is called the Capital. Five similar step-entrance bodies on Dart of Paisley's MAN 11.220s are called the City.

BELOW: *Marshall: The redesigned Dartline body on one of Cambus's short wheelbase Volvo B6s. Note the stepped window line towards the rear.*

Northern Counties Paladin

Built: Wigan, Greater Manchester
Chassis: Dennis Dart, Lance; Volvo B6, B10B, B10M; Scania L113; Leyland Atlantean
Main areas of operation: Greater Manchester, Liverpool, Warrington, Newcastle, Teesside, Dundee, Oxford, Hull, Sussex, Luton, Essex, Leicester, Ipswich, Barnsley

Before 1991, Northern Counties built few single-deckers, but changing circumstances prompted it to develop the 8.5m to 12m Paladin body for rear- and mid-engined chassis. This has deep barrel-shaped windscreens with quarterlights or a double-curvature two-piece windscreen; most have round-edged gasket glazing, but it was also built with square-edged windows. The most unusual are rebodied 10m Atlanteans operated by Blackpool and Merseypride. After Northern Counties came into common ownership with Plaxton in 1995, the midi version was phased out in favour of Plaxton's Pointer, but the 12m body replaced the Plaxton Verde on the final orders for step-entrance Lances.

LEFT: Northern Counties Paladin: A Trent Volvo B10B with the barrel windscreen version of the Paladin.

BELOW: Northern Counties Paladin: A Volvo B6, with double-curvature windscreen, on car park duties at Gatwick Airport.
Northern Counties

Optare

Built: Leeds
Chassis: Leyland Cub, Dennis
Domino, Lance; DAF SB220; MAN
11.180, 11.190; Mercedes-Benz O405
Main areas of operation: London,
Heathrow Airport, Reading, Surrey,
Greater Manchester, Merseyside,
Tyneside, West Midlands, Leicester,
Ipswich, York, Stoke, Aberdeen,
Edinburgh, Brighton, Derby,
Nottingham, Hereford, Co Durham,
Blackpool, Motherwell

When it first took over the old Charles
Roe factory in 1985, Optare developed a
midibus body with a hint of Roe's styling
(including flat vee-shaped windscreens)
for South and West Yorkshire PTEs. South
Yorkshire bought it on 14 Dennis
Domino 7.8m rear-engined midibuses,
short-lived Perkins-engined precursors of
the Dart; West Yorkshire got 15 front-
engined Leyland Cubs. Both batches were
sold fairly soon, but the Cubs, which are
half a bay longer, have been especially long
lived with small operators.

Optare's move into volume full-size bus
bodybuilding began in 1988 with the
Delta, an 11.8m Alusuisse-framed body
on the DAF SB220. It has flat sides with
deep windows and a dramatically styled
front end with a deep curved
windscreen and quarterlights.
It was followed in 1990 by
the 10.1m Vecta on MAN's
11.180 and the 11.190 that

followed it; the Vecta has a more upright
front without quarterlights as, unlike the
DAF, the MAN doesn't have a front
radiator. The 12m Sigma, on the step-
entrance Dennis Lance, was introduced in
1994 (with the Vecta front) and was
followed in 1995 by the Prisma, on the
Mercedes-Benz O.405 and fitted with
Mercedes' own front.

BELOW: *Optare: The original style of
Optare body on a Leyland Cub built for
South Yorkshire PTE. When photographed,
it was owned by Safford's of Great
Gransden, a Cambridgeshire independent
operator.*

RIGHT: *Optare: Barton
Buses, part of the Wellglade
group dominated by Trent, is
the operator of this Delta-
bodied DAF SB220.
Wellglade also operates Vecta-
bodied MANs and Sigma-
bodied Dennis Lances.*
Optare

Plaxton Derwent and Bustler

Built: Scarborough, North Yorkshire
Chassis: Bedford Y-Series; Ford R-Series; AEC Reliance; Leyland Leopard, Tiger; Dennis Javelin; Bristol LH; Scania K112; Volvo B58, B9M, B10M

For many years, Plaxton — like Duple — supplemented coach manufacturing by building rural and interurban service bus bodies mainly in summer when peak demand for coaches had passed.

Its earlier Derwent body, built in the 1960s and 1970s, has a strong BET influence, notably the double-curvature front and rear windscreens and peaked roof domes. West Yorkshire PTE bought them with curved rear domes and a single back window. There is a short side window beside the cab/entrance door on 10m versions and they usually have twin headlamps.

In 1980, this design was replaced by the Bustler, a bus version of the Supreme coach. It has the coach's curved side profile and headlamps from the Supreme IV as well as a BET front windscreen; on high-floor chassis, the side windows are set higher than the cab, running to roof level. Like the Derwent, it has a short window behind the cab/entrance in 10m versions. In a further change, the Bustler was replaced in 1986 by the Derwent 3000 with the same profile and windscreen, but a horizontally divided grille and shallower square-edged side windows that stop short of the roof. It also has a wider destination aperture. A few Derwent 3000s were built on reconditioned Leopard chassis, while First Eastern Counties has several on Dennis Javelins. Production ended around 1990.

BELOW: *Plaxton Derwent: An 11m version of the BET-style Derwent body on a Leyland Leopard operating in Grantham with Reliance of Great Gonerby.*

ABOVE: *Plaxton Derwent: A Scania K112 fitted with a Plaxton Bustler semi-coach body. Highfloor Bustlers have side windows running up to roof height.* **Andrew Jarosz**

BELOW: *Plaxton Derwent 3000: The 3m-high Derwent 3000 on a Yorkshire Rider Leyland Tiger.*

Plaxton Pointer

Built: Scarborough, North Yorkshire; Pilsley, Derbyshire

Chassis: Dennis Dart, Volvo B6

Main areas of operation: Throughout Britain

The Pointer has been astonishingly successful, especially on the Dart. It is an aluminium-framed body developed initially for Plaxton's Reeve Burgess subsidiary which launched it early in 1991. From the outset, it has been built at Scarborough; Reeve Burgess's Pilsley factory closed soon after it went into production. By 1998, around 3,000 had been built.

The original version, on 8.5m, 9m and 9.8m step-entrance Darts, is 2.3m wide and has square-edged gasket glazing which stops short of the bottom of the double-curvature windscreen and cab window; 8.5m and 9.8m versions have a half bay ahead of the rear axle. Stagecoach Oxford bought two-door Pointer Darts. A B6 version, with slightly longer window bays and shallower side windows above the engine compartment, was introduced in 1992; there are far fewer of these —

Mainline, Stagecoach Transit and Travel Dundee are the main operators.

In 1995, lowfloor versions were introduced for both models. Most Pointers on B6LEs have been exported, but the Dart SLF version has been even more successful than the step-entrance model. FirstGroup and Arriva operate large numbers, as do several London operators. It is 2.4m wide, still has gasket glazing as standard and similar front-end mouldings to the original Pointer. The side windows are deeper, running to the same depth as the windscreen and cab window; 10m lowfloor Pointers have the short intermediate bay ahead of the rear axle.

In 1997, the model was relaunched as the Pointer 2 with restyled front and back ends and the option (taken up by FirstGroup) of bonded glazing. The lower front dash has a narrower ventilation duct, with the headlamps and trafficators grouped together; it has roof-level repeater lights at the back. The Super Pointer Dart has Pointer 2 styling, with bonded glazing and a longer rear overhang. A new 8.5m Mini Pointer Dart was announced in 1998.

LEFT: *Plaxton Pointer: A step-entrance Pointer body on a 9.8m Dennis Dart operated by Eastern National in Essex. This carries the fleetname style used before FirstGroup adopted its corporate style with 'f' logo.* **Plaxton**

TOP: *Plaxton Pointer: The first style of lowfloor Pointer on a Dart SLF with Truronian in Cornwall. All but the last two side windows are deeper than on the step-entrance model; the body itself is wider with a more rounded bottom to the lower dash.* **Plaxton**

ABOVE: *Plaxton Pointer: A Pointer 2 for First Provincial in Portsmouth, showing the restyled lower front dash and the optional bonded glazing specified by FirstGroup. Most of the group's buses of this type either have been or will be repainted in its corporate blue, pink and off-white livery. FirstGroup began phasing out prominent local fleetnames in 1998, replacing them with the First name.* **Plaxton**

Plaxton Verde

Built: Scarborough, North Yorkshire
Chassis: Scania N113, Dennis Lance,
Volvo B10B
Main areas of operation: Cardiff,
Swansea, Glasgow, Bristol, Bath, West
Yorkshire, West Midlands, Teesside,
London

The Verde is structurally similar to the Pointer, but outwardly looks quite different mainly because it has a Continental-style two-piece barrel-shaped windscreen and quarterlights. It is also far less common, with only around 300 built. It was launched in 1991 on the Scania N113; 14 are operated by Cardiff Bus, two by First Glasgow and one by Nottingham City Transport; these, and 40 on DAF SB220 chassis for Dublin Bus, have round-edged windows. It was restyled with square-edged gasket glazing from 1993, when delivery of 146 for FirstGroup companies began on Dennis Lance chassis (ordered by the former Badgerline group). Other larger Lance/Verde operators are Stagecoach Selkent and Arriva North West; similar B10B Verdes are operated by Go Ahead in Oxford, by Stagecoach Transit on Teesside, First Citybus in Southampton and by Nottingham. Production was phased out in favour of the more successful Northern Counties Paladin.

BELOW: *Plaxton Verde: A Badgerline Dennis Lance with the second and more common style of Verde body with square-edged gasket-mounted side windows. This is in Badgerline group (pre-FirstGroup) corporate livery with Badger logo on the side and formed part of the only substantial order placed for the Verde; the last buses in the order were fitted with Northern Counties bodies. **Dennis***

Plaxton Prestige

Built: Wigan, Greater Manchester;
Scarborough, North Yorkshire
Chassis: DAF SB220, Volvo B10BLE
Main areas of operation: Heathrow
Airport, London, Greater Manchester,
Birmingham, Tyneside, Chester,
Glasgow

In 1995, Northern Counties unveiled
a prototype 12m lowfloor body on a
DAF SB220 chassis and badged as its
Paladin LF; it had been under
development before the company was
bought by Henlys, Plaxton's owner. A
small batch was built in 1997 on
B10BLEs for Stagecoach Manchester,
and the model was christened the
Plaxton Prestige a little later, when more
DAFs were bodied. Production was
transferred more or less from the outset
from Wigan to Scarborough, although

initial fabrication of some models took
place at Wigan. Early customers
included National Express's Speedlink
company for the shuttle feeder service
from the Heathrow Express rail link at
Heathrow airport, Arriva East Herts &
Essex and London North and Travel
Your Bus in Birmingham. The Prestige
body is also built on the initial deliveries
of LPG-fuelled DAFs. A diesel B10BLE
is operated by First Glasgow.

At first glance, the Prestige looks very
like the Alexander Ultra body on Volvo
B10Ls, especially Ultras with divided
windscreens. Key differences are that
the Plaxton body has flatter sides, its
windscreen is shallower (but has
mouldings to make it appear deeper), its
headlamps and trafficators are closer to
the ground, and the offside emergency
door is farther back.

ABOVE: *Plaxton Prestige: A two-door Prestige, on lowfloor DAF SB220 chassis, in Arriva's
London North fleet. Compare the differences and similarities with the Alexander Ultra-
bodied Volvo B10L illustrated on page 65.* **Plaxton**

94

PMT Knype

Built: Stoke-on-Trent, Staffordshire
Chassis: Leyland Swift, Mercedes-Benz 814
Main areas of operation: Potteries, Chester

PMT Engineering developed the angular Knype body in 1987, the first on a re-engineered Mercedes chassis (see minibus section) with a set-back front axle. More were built in 1989/90 on Swift chassis for the PMT operating company which then was independent of any big group.

LEFT: *PMT Knype: The unmistakably angular and unadorned lines of a Leyland Cub with a Knype body in Chester bus station. First Crosville is the Chester and Wirral division of First PMT; in National Bus Company days, Crosville was one of its largest subsidiaries, covering much of rural Wales and parts of northwest England.*

Reeve Burgess

Built: Pilsley, Derbyshire
Chassis: Dennis Dorchester; Bedford NJM, PJK; Dodge Commando; Leyland Cub, Tiger; MAN-VW MT 8.136
Main area of operation: West Midlands

A Plaxton subsidiary from 1980 until it closed in 1991, Reeve Burgess specialised in small buses and coaches, although it also bodied a 12m Dorchester for Geoff Amos in Northamptonshire. Through the 1980s, it built a standard body which began life with a tall, flat two-piece windscreen, but later gained curved windscreens with space above for a destination display; coach versions were called the Riviera. This body was built on Tayside's 9.5m special Tigers and on a fleet of Cubs operated by Patterson's of Birmingham on social services contracts.

LEFT: *Reeve Burgess: A later example of the Reeve Burgess body on one of Patterson's Leyland Cub CU435s in Birmingham. Compare the chassis layout with the PMT-bodied Cub, as this has the engine mounted directly over the front axle and the entrance behind the axle.*

UVG UrbanStar

Built: Waterlooville, Hampshire
Chassis: Dennis Dart
Main areas of operation: Portsmouth,
Isle of Wight, Southampton,
Gloucester, Irvine, Stirling

The UrbanStar is another product
designed by John Worker. UVG —
standing for Universal Vehicles Group
— bought the former Wadham Stringer
coachbuilding business in 1993 and
revitalised the product range to include
the stainless steel UrbanStar. Its most
distinctive features are the asymmetrical
windscreen which sweeps down in
'teardrop' fashion towards the nearside,

round edges where the otherwise
square-edged side windows sweep up
into the rear section of the bus and
trafficator lights in all four corners of
the roof domes. The first UrbanStars are
operated by First Provincial and an
unusual batch of 8.5m models runs
with Southern Vectis on the Isle of
Wight. A lowfloor version was
introduced in 1996. Production was
suspended before UVG's Waterlooville
operation went into receivership
towards the end of 1997 but was
expected to resume during 1998
following acquisition by Salvador
Caetano.

*LEFT: UVG
UrbanStar: One of
Southern Vectis's 8.5m
step-entrance
UrbanStar-bodied
Dennis Darts at
Newport bus station,
hub of the company's
operations. Southern
Vectis is one of only a
handful of former
National Bus Company
operators to remain
outside the big groups.*
Dennis

Wadham Stringer/WS

Built: Waterlooville, Hampshire
Chassis: Dennis Falcon, Dorchester,
Lancet, Lance, Javelin, Dart; Scania
N112; Bedford Y-Series, PJK, NJM;
Bristol LHS; Leyland Tiger, Cub,
Swift; Volvo B57, B58; Iveco
TurboCity; ACE Cougar
Main areas of operation: Grimsby,
Hartlepool, Eastbourne, Southampton,
Hereford, Kent

Long before it was bought by UVG,

Wadham Stringer built ambulances and
Ministry of Defence vehicles. In 1979,
it entered the bus market with the
Vanguard which sold with modest
success to some municipal fleets. It has
slightly inward-sloping flat sides, deep
side windows with narrow pillars, a
slightly arched double-curvature
windscreen with a more arched roof
dome to accommodate the destination
display, a low horizontal grille and a
small roof pod at the rear.

The Vanguard II, launched in 1986
and particularly popular for a time on

Leyland Swift chassis, has square-edged windows and a more rounded lower dash panel. A coach version for the Swift, called the Winchester, was launched in 1989. It has a single-piece windscreen and non-opening side windows. A solitary example was built on a Dart in 1993. Six Vanguard II bodies went on Iveco TurboCity-U chassis in 1993, around the time of the UVG takeover and when the company changed its name from Wadham Stringer to WS Coachbuilders.

In 1990, Wadham Stringer got ahead of the competition by offering the Portsdown, the first alternative to the Carlyle/Duple Dartline body on the Dart. This, in many ways, was a reaction against some of the least popular features of the Dartline. It is steel framed, with gasket-mounted square-edged windows and a double-curvature divided windscreen. A Portsdown body went on People's Provincial's Perkins-engined ACE Cougar, one of only two of this Yorkshire-made chassis ever built.

ABOVE: *Wadham Stringer Vanguard: One of the original style of Vanguard bodies on a Dennis Lancet in the council-owned Thamesdown fleet in Swindon.*

LEFT: *Wadham Stringer Portsdown: A rare Portsdown body on a short Dennis Dart in the Southampton Citybus fleet.*

Willowbrook Warrior

Built: Loughborough, Leicestershire
Chassis: Leyland Leopard, Tiger;
Bedford Y-Series; ACE Cougar

Willowbrook was a casualty of the 1981 recession, but was re-formed on a smaller scale in 1985, building bus and coach bodies for about five or six years, mainly on reconditioned chassis. The Warrior, which looks a little like the Leyland Lynx, but has flat windscreens and gasket glazing, had a brief following that included South Wales and Scottish independents and some larger operators like Oxford Bus and Brighton Buses. The other ACE Cougar has a Warrior body.

LEFT: *Willowbrook Warrior: A Leyland Leopard rebodied with a Warrior bus body. When photographed in 1991, it was operating with Oxford Bus; since the Go Ahead group took over, these vehicles have become driver training vehicles with group subsidiary Brighton & Hove.*

Wright Handybus

Built: Ballymena, Co Antrim
Chassis: Dennis Dart, Leyland Swift
Main areas of operation: London, Welwyn Garden City, Hemel Hempstead, South Wales, Tyne & Wear, Walsall, Staffordshire, Belfast

Before the Handybus was launched in 1990, Wright's built mainly for its home market in Northern Ireland, although it also sold a few rather utilitarian looking buses and the stylish Contour coach described later in this book. A move to a new factory prompted substantial expansion which was rewarded in the early stages by several large orders from London. Like all Wright's buses built from around 1978, the Handybus uses the Alusuisse structural system. This body met London's requirements and has a retro look of a 1950s bus, with a square profile, flat front and either two separate front windscreens with the driver's screen raked back to reduce reflection, or else a single-piece flat windscreen. Outside London, Handybus operators include Go Ahead North East, Stagecoach Rhondda, Travel West Midlands, Arriva's The Shires subsidiary and Universitybus. When it was an independent company, Arriva's Stevenson fleet in Staffordshire bought four with high-floor Leyland Swift chassis. Like most Wright's bodies, the Handybus has a W-shaped moulding between the headlamps; operators often pick this out in a contrasting colour.

ABOVE: *Wright Handybus: A 9.8m Handybus with the original style of separate windscreens. The raked driver's screen harks back to buses of the 1950s. This is on a Dennis Dart operated by what was Luton & District, then became The Shires and now is part of the Arriva empire. It was operating town services in Hemel Hempstead.*

ABOVE: *Wright Handybus: The quartet of Leyland Swifts with Handybus bodies look quite odd compared with the more common Dart versions, as they have taller fronts and narrow track front axles. They have the single-piece windscreen also fitted on many Darts. Stevenson's now trades as Arriva Midlands North.* **Wright's**

Wright Endeavour, Endurance, Urbanranger, Pathfinder, Liberator, Crusader, Renown, Axcess-ultralow and Axcess Floline

Built: Ballymena, Co Antrim
Chassis: Dennis Dart SLF, Lance SLF; Volvo B6LE, B10B, B10BLE, B10L; Scania K93, N113, L113, L94; Mercedes-Benz OH1416, O405; Leyland Tiger
Main areas of operation: London, Heathrow Airport, Bristol airport, Essex, Hertfordshire, Tyneside, Bath, Aberdeen, Edinburgh, Dundee, Glasgow, Greater Manchester, Merseyside, West Midlands, Harrogate, West Yorkshire, Barnsley, York, South Wales, Brighton, Oxford, Northern Ireland

Wright's dramatically changed the style of its bodies in May 1992 with the Endeavour, an express coach body built on 25 of the last Leyland Tigers for Ulsterbus. This introduced a new look with double-curvature windscreens, a more rounded lower front dash incorporating the W-shaped mouldings and tall side windows. It was followed four months later by the first five Endurance bus bodies, on Scania K93 chassis for Yorkshire Traction. Many more Endurances, with slightly lower bodies and shorter side windows, followed on B10Bs for fleets including MTL, Greater Manchester North (First Manchester today), Travel West Midlands, West Riding, Blazefield's Harrogate, Keighley and Sovereign (Hertfordshire) operations

ABOVE: *Wright Crusader: Over 150 Volvo B6LEs, with 10.6m Wright's Crusader lowfloor midibus body, are operated by Travel West Midlands and its sister Travel Dundee fleet. This example, in West Bromwich, has gasket-glazed windows. Travel West Midlands is the largest bus operating subsidiary of the National Express Group which also runs coach services, train franchises and airports.* ***Wright's***

and CMT Buses in Liverpool. Most have gasket glazing, but the Manchester vehicles have bonded windows. Endurances with bonded glazing were built on Scania N113 chassis for First Midland Bluebird in Scotland. Others with Mercedes fronts, on O.405 chassis, are operated by First Aberdeen and Midland Bluebird (with gasket and bonded windows). A shortened version, with Wright's front and a Mercedes badge in place of the W-mouldings, is fitted on OH1416 Urban-rangers.

Wright's kick-started the lowfloor revolution in 1993 with the Pathfinder body on Lance SLF and Scania N113 chassis. Outwardly, it is very similar to the Endurance and all have bonded glazing. The lowfloor body is called the Axcess-ultralow on the L113, the Axcess Floline on the L94, Liberator on the B10L, Renown on the B10BLE and Crusader on the smaller B6LE and Dart SLF. One useful identification feature is that the rear number plate and destination display are at the top of the back window on the Liberator, Renown and B10B Endurance; they are at the bottom of the back window on the Axcess-ultralow, Axcess Floline and Scania-chassised Endurance. The Renown, Crusader and Axcess Floline are available with gasket glazing; Floline is a Wright brand name for a sloping floor that carries extra strength enabling gasket glazing to be fitted. Wright's 12m lowfloor bodies are standard equipment for FirstGroup fleets, and 18m articulated buses have been ordered for 1998/9.

BELOW: *Wright Renown: A 12m Wright Renown 47-seater, on Volvo B10BLE chassis, in First Badgerline livery. The blue, pink and off-white FirstGroup livery — nicknamed 'Barbie buses' because they look like the colours of best-selling children's dolls — are being applied to the group's newest buses with purple and green interiors. FirstGroup specifies bonded glazing on most of its buses, including this vehicle, but the Renown and Axcess Floline (Scania L94) are available with gasket glazing.* **Wright's**

Coaches are most readily identified by their bodywork, although manufacturers' badges and a few tell-tale features like engine position and radiators (eg for the latest series of Volvo B10M and the Dennis Javelin) will help tell you which chassis is fitted. The most common types of coach in British fleets are listed in this section, but a few rare and older types have been omitted. Earlier editions of *abc Bus & Coach Recognition* have details of some of these.

As indicated in Part 2, all mid- and front-engined chassis except for the Leyland DAB have also been bodied as coaches; so have the MAN 11.180, 190 and 220 (and the similar 10.180), Scania K92, K93 and L94 and a few early Volvo B6s and B6Rs. Chassis built exclusively as coaches are listed below:

Rear-Engined

DAF SB2300/2305
Built: Eindhoven, Netherlands 1980-92
Engine: DAF 8.25-litre
Transmission: ZF synchromesh or automatic
Length: 12m two-axle

DAF SB3000
Built: Eindhoven, Netherlands 1985 to date
Engine: DAF WS242 11.6-litre
Transmission: ZF synchromesh or automatic
Length: 12m two- or three-axle

Iveco EuroRider 391.12.29 and 391.12.35
Built: Barcelona, Spain 1995 to date
Engine: Iveco 8460.41S 9.5-litre (290 and 345hp)
Transmission: ZF synchromesh or automatic
Length: 12m two-axle

MAN 16.290, 18.310, 24.400
Built: Salzgitter, Germany 1989 to date
Engine: MAN D2066 12-litre
Transmission: ZF synchromesh or automatic
Length: 12m two- and (24.400) three-axle

Mercedes-Benz O.303, OH.1628L
Built: Mannheim, Germany 1975-91
Engine: Mercedes OM402 V8 (OM422 V8 on 1628L)
Transmission: Mercedes synchromesh or automatic; ZF synchromesh
Length: 12m two-axle

Scania K113/K124
Built: Katrineholm, Sweden 1988 to date (K113), 1997 to date (K124)
Engine: Scania DSC11 (K113) 11-litre, DSC12 (K124) 12-litre
Transmission: Scania synchromesh or automatic
Length: 12m two- or three-axle

Volvo B7R
Built: Borås, Sweden 1997 to date
Engine: Volvo D7B 7-litre
Transmission: ZF synchromesh or automatic
Length: 12m two-axle

Volvo B12T

Built: Borås, Sweden 1993 to date
Engine: Volvo D12 12-litre
Transmission: Volvo automatic
Length: 12m three-axle

Mid-Engined

DAF MB200/MB230

Built: Eindhoven, Netherlands
1975-93
Engine: DAF 11.6-litre
Transmission: ZF synchromesh or
automatic
Length: 11m or 12m two-axle

Front-Engined

Iveco EuroMidi 80 and 95

Built: Brescia, Italy 1994 to date
Engine: Iveco 8060.45B 5.9-litre
Transmission: Iveco synchromesh,
Allison automatic
Length: 8.5m and 9.3m two-axle

Mercedes-Benz O1120L

Built: Wörth, Germany (for UK) 1997
to date
Engine: Mercedes OM366LA 211hp
Transmission: Mercedes synchromesh
Length: 9.2m two-axle

Coach Bodies and Integrals

Berkhof

Built: Valkenswaard, Netherlands

Chassis: AEC Reliance; DAF SB2300, 3000, MB200; Dennis Dorchester, Javelin; Leyland Tiger; Scania K92, K112, K113; Volvo B10M; MAN 11.180, 11.190, 11.220

Berkhof bodies, built by a company that now also owns Jonckheere, were first imported to Britain in 1982 by Ensign Bus Sales in Essex and sold especially well to operators in and around Greater London. The range imported then all have the same basic outline, with a raked windscreen and an upswept grille and headlamp assembly. The best seller was the 3.4m- and 3.5m-high Esprite with either horizontally or vertically divided windscreen; less common now are the 3.95m Emperor — with the main seating area above the driver and an additional seating saloon behind the rear axle — and the 4m-high Eclipse double-decker.

The 1987 Excellence range was introduced to the UK in 1989 on Scania, Volvo, MAN and Dennis Javelin chassis when AVE Berkhof took over the franchise. This has a revised front end with twin recessed headlamps. The 3.3m Excellence 1000 has a single-piece windscreen; the 3.7m 2000 has a horizontally divided two-piece windscreen, the top part of which rakes sharply to give a hint of Neoplan styling; there also is a 4m-high 3000 double-decker — the first of which was imported on a DAF SB3000.

A new range came in from 1996, starting with the Axial which replaced the Excellence 2000 and has a raked front and a slight bulge in the roof above the windscreen. It was followed in 1997 by the Excellence 1000's replacement, the 2.55m-wide, 3.3m-high Radial with an upright front. On both models, the frontmost side windows sweep down towards the level of the bottom of the windscreen.

ABOVE: *Berkhof: A low driving position Berkhof Esprite body on a Volvo B10M chassis. When built on chassis with a higher driving position, it has a vertically divided windscreen. Like many older coaches, the Berkhof's age has been disguised by a dateless number plate — in this case a Northern Ireland registration.*

ABOVE: *Berkhof: A 3.7m-high Excellence 2000 body on a Scania K113 chassis, operating on the Berks Bucks Bus Company's Reading-Heathrow Railair Link service.*

ABOVE: *Berkhof: A short wheelbase Dennis Javelin with a Berkhof Excellence 1000 body — a body style also fitted on rear-engined MAN midicoaches.*

ABOVE: *Berkhof: A 12m Javelin with the newer Axial body operating for Expressway of Rotherham.* **Dennis**

Beulas

Built: Arbucies, Spain 1995 to date
Chassis: Iveco EuroRider

Beulas (pronounced 'Beelass') is a long-established Spanish coachbuilder selected as sole supplier of bodies for the right-hand-drive EuroRider which has been sold with increasing success in the UK. It entered the market with the 3.42m-high Stergo E which has front side windows sweeping down to line up with the base of the windscreen and is available on EuroRider 29 and 35 models; it was joined in 1997 by the IntaLina, a 3.22m-high body with a straight window line. Both have a raked, rounded front; on the higher body, the Iveco badge is in a lozenge-shaped moulding between the headlamps.

LEFT: Beulas Stergo: An Iveco EuroRider 35 with the 3.42m-high Stergo body fitted on most of these coaches since their UK launch in 1995. The lower height IntaLina body has straight side windows.

Bova Europa

Built: Valkenswaard, Netherlands 1981-3
Engine: DAF 8.25-litre
Transmission: ZF synchromesh, Allison automatic

The integral Bova was one of the first successful imports of a rear-engined Continental coach to Britain and sold well to operators which previously bought lightweight Fords and Bedfords. The front axle has a narrower track than the rear axle. The Europa underframe was also bodied by Duple.

BELOW: Bova Europa: The Europa's curved front and flat sides give it an unmistakable look. The DAF badge above the offside headlamp refers to the engine. This one was working for a Suffolk coach tour operator when photographed in 1993.

Bova Futura

Built: Valkenswaard, Netherlands
1983 to date
Engines: DAF 11.6-litre, 8.65-litre
RS200; Mercedes-Benz; Cummins 6CT
Transmission: ZF synchromesh or
automatic

The Europa gave way to the more
powerful and radically styled 3.3m- and
3.5m-high Futura. It is more
aerodynamic, thanks to its raked
windscreen and bulbous front dash
panel which tucks back into the
bottom. There are very few Mercedes-
powered Futuras. The Cummins option
was introduced for the UK after Optare
became one of Bova's UK dealers; it and
the RS200 are fitted in interurban
Futuras.

*LEFT: Bova Futura:
The Futura has an
even more
unmistakable
appearance, with its
bulbous front end
which is very much a
trademark of this
Dutch coach design.*

Caetano

Built: Oporto, Portugal
Chassis: Volvo B10M, B6; DAF
MB200/230, SB2300, SB3000;
Dennis Dorchester, Javelin; MAN
10.180, 11.180, 11.190, 11.220; Ford
R-Series

Salvador Caetano led
the march of imported
coaches to Britain back
in 1968. The square-
profile Alpha was sold
from 1978 to 1982 and
was followed in 1983 by
the Algarve body. Early

Algarves have arrow-shaped vertical slats
on the grille; by 1986, the slats were
horizontal. In 1991, the Algarve II, with
upswept cab and entrance door glazing,
was launched. In 1995, the Porto was
introduced exclusively on the Dennis
Javelin, but was discontinued following

*RIGHT: Caetano Alpha:
An example of the square-
profile Alpha on a mid-
engined DAF MB230
chassis.* **Andrew Jarosz**

LEFT: *Caetano Algarve: One of the later versions of the Mk1 Algarve, with more restrained grille design. This is on a Dennis Javelin chassis — identifiable by the grille ahead of the rear wheel.*

Caetano's purchase of UVG in 1998. The Porto has a similar outline to the Algarve, but at 3.2m is lower than the lowest (3.35m) Algarve and is intended for dual-purpose bus-cum-coach work; it has gasket glazing.

In 1997, a prototype Enigma — available, like the Algarve II, on B10M and Javelin chassis — was unveiled. It is 3.5m high with a downswept roof and side windows towards the front.

LEFT: *Caetano Algarve II: Lothian, the largest surviving council-owned bus company, operates this Algarve II-bodied Javelin in its coach fleet.* **Dennis**

LEFT:
Caetano Enigma: The first Enigma for the British market was shown at Coach & Bus '97 on a Volvo B10M chassis. Production versions have deeper windscreens arched at top and bottom to match the shape of the roof.

Drögmöller

Built: Heilbronn, Germany 1984-6
Engine: Mercedes-Benz 280hp
Transmission: ZF synchromesh

Drögmöller is one of the most exclusive coach manufacturers in Europe. It virtually hand-builds very expensive, high quality integral coaches mainly for its home market in Germany, and before it was taken over by Volvo in 1994 — and began fitting B12 running units — it installed Mercedes engines, axles and brakes. Only three have been sold in Britain. The first, an E330 Comet exhibited at the 1984 Motor Show, has unusual theatre-style seating which slopes up to the back to give every passenger an uninterrupted view ahead; the side windows follow the angle of the floor. This coach was bought by Bergland International of Watford which went on to buy two E320 Euro Pullman models in 1986. They have a more conventional layout with a level floor set higher than the driver. All three have the same arrow-shaped windows behind the cab/entrance. These coaches, and Bergland's business, have since been bought by Ebdon's of Sidcup, Kent.

LEFT:
Drögmöller: Two-thirds of the British population of Drögmöllers in one photograph. On the left is one of the two E320 Euro Pullmans; on the right is the only E330 Comet — with theatre-style seating — brought to Britain.

Duple Dominant

Built: Blackpool, Lancashire
Chassis: AEC Reliance; Bedford VAS/PJK, SB/NJM, Y-Series; Bristol LH; Dennis Falcon (Goldliner only); Ford R-Series; Leyland Leopard, Tiger; Volvo B58, B10M; DAF MB200

Once Britain's leading coach builder, Duple declined from the late 1960s until it sold most of its business to Plaxton in 1989. It fought back against Plaxton in 1972 by launching the steel-framed Dominant — a full two years before its arch rival began to phase out composite (metal and wood) framing. The Dominant has a similar shape to Plaxton's bow-sided Elite (it was largely designed by the same person); it has brightwork window surrounds (usually including a ribbed section under the windows) and, in its original form, interchangeable front and rear divided windscreens. A bus-seated version, the Dominant E, was offered from 1975 with less brightwork; both models were available with a 'Bristol dome' destination display (so called after Plaxton bodied some Bristol REs for

National Bus Company subsidiaries) above the windscreen.

The Michelotti-styled Dominant II, with deeper windscreen, restyled grille (also used on later versions of the original model) and shallower back window was available from 1976 on underfloor-engined coaches and, from 1977, on inclined-engined Fords.

To meet the Scottish Bus Group's requirements for overnight coaches, the Dominant III followed in 1980. It has small, forward-sloping trapezoid windows. At the same time, the Dominant IV, with shallower standard windows and much less brightwork, was added to the range. Goldliner high-floor versions of the Dominant II, III and IV, with roofline stepped either behind the cab/entrance or run straight through from behind a raised destination screen,

were launched in 1981, a year before Dominant production ended.

There were further variations: Dominant II, III and IV with Dominant I windscreens; Dominant II with Dominant I back window; and Dominant II side windows in the front half and Dominant IV windows towards the back. Flat glasses were also available and some SBG Dominant IIIs were rebuilt with Dominant II and IV side windows.

Standard specification included a single-piece inward-hinged door, but some Goldliners have outward-opening plug doors and, for local service work, the Dominant Express specification incorporates two-leaf doors either all-glass or, on later models, with four separate window panes.

BELOW: Duple Dominant II: A Ford R1114 with Dominant II body operated by TransLinc, a now privatised transport company formed by Lincolnshire County Council, with a Duple 320-bodied Dennis Javelin behind.

LEFT: *Duple Dominant III: The forward-sloping trapezoid windows clearly distinguish the Dominant III, here on a Bedford Y-Series operating in Darlington in 1991.*

Duple Laser, Caribbean and Calypso

Built: Blackpool, Lancashire
Chassis: Bedford Y-Series; Leyland Tiger; Volvo B10M; DAF MB200; Dennis Dorchester; Bova

The Dominant was followed by the Laser and Caribbean which lasted from 1982 to 1985, a period that spanned the takeover of the company by Dennis's then parent, Hestair. The new lowfloor successor, the Laser, is a more rounded design with a distinct Dominant look about it. For its first two years, it was built with a divided windscreen and gasket glazing; for its final year it got a single-piece windscreen, a revised grille and bonded glazing. When fitted, destination displays are at the top of the windscreen. Lasers were built only on Bedford, Leyland and Volvo chassis.

The Goldliner's successor was the Caribbean, a much flatter design with square-edged windows from the outset and a deep windscreen; it was also fitted on DAF and Dennis chassis. For its last year, the Caribbean got a restyled grille and bonded glazing. In 1984/5, Duple also built the Calypso, a lowheight Caribbean, on Bova chassis with narrow track front axles; it has five window bays instead of the Caribbean's six.

BELOW: *Duple Laser: A Volvo B10M with the later version of Duple Laser body with bonded glazing and a single-piece windscreen.*

111

ABOVE: *Duple Caribbean: An Ulsterbus DAF MB230 with the later version of the Caribbean body passing some of the brash trappings of Blackpool seafront.*

ABOVE: *Duple Calypso: A Calypso-bodied Bova in the coach park at South Mimms services in Hertfordshire, at the interchange of the A1(M) and M25. The body is lower than the Caribbean and has fewer window bays.*

Duple 425

Built: Blackpool, Lancashire 1985-89;
Fourchambault, France 1992

Engines: Cummins L10; DAF 10.6-
litre

Transmission: ZF synchromesh or
automatic

When Hestair bought Duple in 1983,
it was building a prototype integral
Caribbean on a Neoplan chassis and the
project developed into the distinctive
12m integral 425 which was launched
in 1984, a year before production
began. It was designed by John Worker,
who has since designed bus bodies for
Alexander, East Lancs and UVG, and
was the first British bus or coach to use
Cromweld stainless steel. It has air
suspension and a rear engine; to achieve
the 0.425 drag coefficient from which
the model number is taken, the deep
windscreen rakes back sharply into the
roof dome. Three were exported to
Switzerland and, after Plaxton bought
Duple's designs in 1989, it was re-
engineered ready for 12 to be built
(badged as Plaxton 425s) at the
company's Carrosserie Lorraine plant in
France shortly before it was closed.

ABOVE: *Duple 425: Duple created a strikingly different look with the John Worker-designed 425. Note the sharply raked upper windscreen section.*

Duple 320/340 (and Plaxton 321)

Built: Blackpool, Lancashire;
Scarborough, North Yorkshire
Chassis: Bedford Y-Series; Leyland
Tiger; Volvo B10M; DAF MB, SB;
Scania K93; Dennis Javelin

The Laser and Caribbean were
succeeded by the 3.2m-high 320 and
the 3.4m 340, both of which bear a
passing resemblance to the Caribbean.
They have bonded glazing and either
single or divided windscreens; the 340's
unglazed front roof dome has a hint of
the 425, but is much less dramatic. At
the end of 1990, Plaxton built 25 320
bodies, all on Tiger chassis, badged as
the Plaxton 321 and with Plaxton-
designed interiors, wheel arch and side
mouldings.

BELOW: *Duple 320: A Duple 320, with straight roof.*

ABOVE: *Duple 340: A Duple 340 operating with Chiltern Queens, a long-established Berkshire coach and bus operator.*

ECW B51

Built: Lowestoft, Suffolk.
Chassis: Leyland Leopard, Tiger.

ECW revived a 1970 coach body style in 1982 when it bodied 155 Leopards and Tigers for the National Bus Company. The B51 was influenced by Plaxton styling, but has flat side windows. The destination box is incorporated into the top of the windscreen and, when new, the area below the windscreen was painted matt black to create the illusion of deeper glazing. Structural problems plagued these vehicles as the body was designed originally for the Bristol RE and had insufficient strength in the back of a mid-engined coach; many have been scrapped or rebodied.

BELOW: ECW B51: Surviving B51 coaches are scattered far and wide. This Leyland Leopard, new to Eastern Counties, was operating from Dumfries when photographed in 1995. When new, the moulding below the windscreen — which includes the MacEwan fleetname — would have been painted matt black to make the windscreen look much deeper.
Murdoch Currie

FAP-Sanos S315.21 Charisma

Built: Skopje, Yugoslavia
Engine: Mercedes-Benz OM442 V8
Transmission: ZF synchromesh

The Charisma is a low-cost version of the Mercedes O303, licence-built in Yugoslavia. Ensign Bus Sales imported it in 1989/90 after severing ties with Berkhof, selling it at around two-thirds of the price of the German original. It is barely distinguishable from a 'real' O303, save for the badging where operators have left it in place. Even then, some operators replaced the circular front badge with an identical size Mercedes star.

ABOVE: *Charisma: Only the rather anonymous-looking badge between the headlamps and the sliding bottom halves of two of the side windows show that this is a Charisma and not a genuine German-built Mercedes O.303. This was one of several operated by Hamilton Services of Uxbridge on National Express duplicate journeys.*

Ikarus

Built: Budapest, Hungary
Chassis: Volvo B10M, DAF SB3000

Ikarus's first foray in the UK market came in 1987 when the Kirkby coach and bus dealership imported the first of 101 Blue Danube bodies designed for western markets. These were all built on Volvo chassis and the deal was reached before Kirkby management bought Plaxton. This 3.6m-high body has bowed side windows, a tall windscreen and a front dash that tucks in towards the bottom. The last entered service in 1991, but Hughes DAF (now Arriva Bus & Coach) revived the design for the British market in 1995 by offering it as a lower-cost option on the rear-engined DAF SB3000. Two models, the 3.25m-high 350 and the 3.55m-high 396, are offered; they lack the lower grille fitted in the Volvo version.

BELOW: *Ikarus: A London Coaches DAF SB3000 with Ikarus 350 body on London's Victoria Embankment while on one of the company's commuter services to North Kent. Ikarus Volvos have a grille in the panel below the front number plate.*

Indcar

Built: Arbucies, Spain
Chassis: Iveco
EuroMidi

Indcar — short for Industrial Carrocera Arbuciense — is a Spanish midibus and coach builder. The 35-seat Eco body on the EuroMidi 95 looks a little like a scaled down

version of the Beulas body built nearby on the 12m EuroRider. The Eco-3 was succeeded by the Eco-4 in 1997; the main visual differences are its wider grille, round headlamps instead of square and 'rabbit ear' wing mirrors hung from the top front corners. At the same time, Iveco also began importing the 29-seat Maxim body on the shorter EuroMidi 80. It is aimed at the sector of the market that used to buy the Bedford PJK, but could hardly look more different, with a sharply raked front and large windscreen.

ABOVE: Indcar Eco-3: One of the first Indcar-bodied Iveco EuroMidi 95 coaches for a British operator was this Eco-3 for Hodgsons Private Hire of Barnard Castle. The Eco-4 has a wider grille, round headlamps and wing mirrors hung from the top corners of the windscreen pillars. **Iveco Bus**

BELOW: Indcar Maxim: The striking-looking Maxim body on the EuroMidi 80 is designed to be so different that people will want to travel in it. It certainly is unmistakable. **Iveco Bus**

Irizar

Built: Ormaiztegui, Spain
Chassis: Volvo B58, B10M; Scania
K113, K124, L94; MAN 11.220

Irizar (pronounced 'Ireethar') bodies were first imported from the Basque country in 1979, but have become much more common through a tie-up with Scania from 1993. The original body, the Urko, is a striking design with a raised seating area and roof in the rear half. It was followed from 1983 by the plainer 3.5m Pyrenean and 3.4m Shetland models which sold in very small numbers.

In 1993, Scania set up an exclusive deal to import Irizar's Century body to the UK, based initially on four- and six-wheel K113s. This coach has a high level of standard equipment, including air conditioning, and the 3.5m-high body has a stepped-down front with a thick pillar behind the downward-sloping front side window. A lower body, the InterCentury, was introduced from 1997 on the then new L94

(examples are operated by FirstGroup in Glasgow) and Scania also sells a midi version based on the MAN chassis as there is no equivalent Scania product.

BELOW: *Irizar Urko: Another unique design to come out of northern Spain was the Urko, brought to Britain on Volvo B58 chassis. Both the coach and the car behind have cherished number plates.*

BOTTOM:
Irizar Century: Redwoods, a Devon coach operator, adopted an American-style livery for this Irizar Century on six-wheel Scania K113 chassis.

Jonckheere

Built: Roeselare, Belgium
Chassis: Bedford Y-Series; Volvo B58,
B10M, B12T; Scania K92, K112;
Leyland Tiger; DAF SB, MB; Dennis
Lancet; MAN 11.180, 11.190, 11.220,
16.290, 24.400; Mercedes-Benz
O.303, OH1628L

Jonckheere (pronounced 'Yonk here')
has been building for the UK since the
early 1970s and most seriously since
1980. It has been owned by Berkhof
since 1994, but continues to build a
separate range of products.

The high-floor Bermuda, with large
rectangular grille and the manufacturer's
'J' badge, was produced until 1982. It
was superseded by the Jubilee range
with a shallower grille, square
headlamps and a curved windscreen.
The base model P50 is 3.5m high with
a vertically divided windscreen; the
P599 has a lower driving position and a
deeper, horizontally divided
windscreen, the lower half of which may
be divided vertically; the 4m-high four-
wheel P90 and six-wheel P95 have a
rear saloon behind the back axle; the
4m P99 double-decker was built on
three-axle Scania and DAF SB chassis.

There also was a P35 Piccolo midicoach
and six Scania K92 buses were supplied
in 1986 with a low version of the P50
body. In 1989, the Jubilee was replaced
by the P599 Deauville (on Volvo, DAF,
MAN and Mercedes chassis) and P99
Monaco (MAN, DAF and Volvo B12T)
which have a restyled front without the
'J' logo. In 1998, Stagecoach ordered 27
Monacos, on MAN 24.400 chassis, for
its London-Oxford Tube service.

The Mistral, with raked front, large
single-piece windscreen and heavy pillar
behind the first window bay giving it
the look of the Irizar Century, was
launched in 1995; Stagecoach acquired
two articulated versions in 1996, on
B10M chassis, for its express routes in
Scotland and has ordered more for
1999. It is one of the first UK customers
for the Modulo, a lower height body
with an upright front, straight side
window line and a 'smiling' effect
moulding incorporating the headlamps
and lower front dash.

BELOW: *Jonckheere: The position of the
grille on this Bermuda-bodied Volvo makes
the windscreen appear to be shallower than
it is.*

LEFT: *Jonckheere: A Jubilee P50-bodied Volvo B10M with the bodybuilder's 'J' logo above the Volvo badge.*

LEFT: *Jonckheere: A Monaco double-decker on Volvo B12T chassis. Similar coaches, on MAN 24.400 chassis, have been ordered by Stagecoach Oxford.* **Author's collection**

LEFT: *Jonckheere: One of the first two articulated Mistrals, on Volvo B10M chassis, for Stagecoach working on one of Fife Scottish's express services.*

LAG Panoramic, EOS

Built: Bree, Belgium
Engines: DAF
11.6-litre,
Cummins L10
Transmission: ZF
synchromesh

LAG, owned by the Goossens family, entered the British market in 1982, selling its raked-front Galaxy body on Volvo, DAF and Leyland mid-engined chassis, but it had turned to its own integrals by 1987,

BELOW: *LAG Panoramic: By comparison with what followed, the LAG Panoramic had quite a restrained appearance. This was one of several operated by Suffolk operator Belle Coaches of Leiston.*

selling the Panoramic usually with a DAF engine and which has an upright, horizontally divided windscreen. In 1989, it moved to a new factory and replaced the Panoramic with the DAF-engined 3.6m-high EOS, which has independent front suspension, separate upper and lower windscreens and a deep black area below the lower windscreen to create the illusion of more glass. LAG was overstretched by the move and was sold to Van Hool in 1990. The EOS has been developed as a separate range, details of which appear under the Van Hool heading.

BELOW: *LAG EOS: The separate windscreens and thick pillars around the upper windscreen help identify the LAG EOS. The black area beneath the lower windscreen makes it appear deeper. The coach alongside is an MAN 16.290 with Jonckheere Deauville body.*

Leyland Royal Tiger Doyen

Built: Leeds 1982-84; Workington, Cumbria 1983-87
Engines: Leyland TL11H, Cummins L10
Transmission: ZF synchromesh or automatic; Leyland automatic

The rear-engined Royal Tiger was Leyland's final answer to the flood of foreign coaches which hit the UK market from around 1979. When bodied in-house, 42 by Roe and 56 at Workington, it was given the Doyen suffix. The Doyen body has a deep, raked windscreen made to appear even deeper by black ribbed moulding beneath it. The bonded side windows curve sharply at the top. A further 65 Royal Tiger underframes were bodied by Plaxton and Van Hool and can be identified by air intakes around the engine compartment. Volvo axed the Royal Tiger when it bought Leyland Bus in 1988, production having already been suspended by lack of orders.

BELOW: *Leyland Royal Tiger Doyen: The crowned tiger badge on the grille completes the striking appearance of this less than commercially successful British coach.*

MAN SR280

Built: Salzgitter, Germany (for UK) 1979-85
Chassis: Dennis Javelin, MAN 18.310
Engines: MAN 11.4 litre
Transmission: ZF synchromesh

The flat-sided SR280 was the first high specification rear-engined Continental coach offered in quantity to UK operators. It was offered in higher and lower forms with a choice of vertically-divided or one-piece windscreens. the rectangular grille is an MAN trademark.

ABOVE RIGHT: *MAN SR280: MAN stormed into the market with the SR280, only to lose enthusiasm after its importership changed hands. The body design is unique and may have helped influence Duple's design of its Caribbean and Calypso.*

Marcopolo Explorer

Built: Coimbra, Portugal
Chassis: Dennis Javelin, MAN 18.310

Brazilian-based Marcopolo is one of the world's largest bus and coach bodybuilders. In 1991, it bought a small Portuguese coachbuilding company and, three years later, began developing a European version of the Viaggio intercity coach sold in Brazil since 1992. This came to Britain in 1995, as the Explorer, selling in small volumes on Javelin chassis. It has a large curved windscreen reminiscent of the Wright Contour of the 1980s.

BELOW: *Marcopolo: Some of the first Marcopolo Explorer-bodied Dennis Javelins were bought by Hamilton Services of Uxbridge.*

MCW Metroliner

Built: Birmingham 1982-7
Engines: Cummins L10, Gardner
6LYT
Transmission: ZF synchromesh, Voith
or ZF automatic

MCW launched itself into the coach market in 1982 with the 12m bonded-glazed Metroliner, building 130 double-deckers and 42 single-deckers.

Most common was the 4.2m-high three-axle double-decker with transverse Cummins engine and Voith gearbox. There were one- and two-door versions with either front or centre staircases and a large rear luggage area. Most operated with National Bus Company subsidiaries, but all survivors now run with subsequent owners — some as open-top London sightseeing buses. The last three double-deckers, built in 1986/7, were fully integral 4m-high 400GT models with longitudinal Gardner engines and heavily raked fronts.

All the single-deckers had longitudinal L10 engines. Half were 3.2m models with separate chassis; half were integral 3.4m Hi-Liners. The first 11 of the 3.2m Metroliners had square flat-sided bodies with bonded glazing and a slightly curved asymmetrical windscreen. The rest had a restyled body with curved sides and a raked windscreen; the Hi-Liner has a separate panel for the destination display above the windscreen, as well as a deeper panel above the entrance door.

RIGHT: MCW Metroliner: A double-deck Metroliner new to NBC's West Yorkshire Road Car and operating with Provence Private Hire of St Albans. This is a one-door 79-seater with its staircase directly behind the driver's cab; two-door Metroliners have rear staircases.

LEFT: MCW Metroliner: PPH bought most of the surviving single-deck coaches. This Hi-Liner was new to Wessex, one of NBC's coaching subsidiaries and now part of FirstGroup.

Mercedes-Benz O.303

Built: Mannheim, Germany 1975-90
Engine: Mercedes OM442 V8
Transmission: Mercedes synchromesh

Mercedes-Benz, the vehicle manufacturing division of German industrial group Daimler-Benz, first brought its integral rear-engined O.302 to Britain in 1967 and made various attempts to sell the O.303 here, either with its own bodywork or bodied by coachbuilding specialists like Jonckheere

and Plaxton. In 1985, it began a more serious effort to sell high- and lowfloor complete O.303s, and followed that in 1990 with a single run of 25 with Plaxton Paramount 3500 bodies. The Mercedes body — the original from which the FAP-Sanos Charisma was copied — is a familiar sight across Europe, with short curved side windows, deep single-piece or divided windscreen and a front dash with a prominent three-pointed star logo. O.303 production transferred to Russia in 1991.

Mercedes-Benz O.404 Vita

Built: Mannheim, Germany (for UK) 1997 to date

Engine: Mercedes OM441LA V6.
Transmission: Mercedes synchromesh or ZF automatic

Although the integral O404 was launched in left-hand-drive markets in 1991, Mercedes held back from launching a right-hand-drive version for Britain. Instead, in 1997 it introduced the O404.15.RHD with bodywork built in Zaragoza, Spain by Hispano Carrocera, a Mexican-owned company which began life in 1955 as Van Hool's Spanish subsidiary. In line with Mercedes' policy of moving away from numbers to model names, it is called Vita (not to be confused with a Spanish-built Mercedes van called the Vito). Contemporary fashion has given it swept-down side windows directly behind the cab/entrance, with the passenger door glazed almost from top to bottom; it has a more upright front than Irizar and Beulas coaches.

Neoplan

Built: Stuttgart and Berlin, Germany (for UK) 1980 to date

Engines: Mercedes OM422 V8, OM423 V10, OM402LA, OM401LA; Gardner 6LYT; Cummins N14; Scania DS11; DAF 11.6-litre; MAN D2866; also Dennis Javelin and MAN 18.350 chassis
Transmission: (integrals) ZF synchro-mesh or automatic; Scania automatic, Allison automatic

The highly individual Neoplan range of integral rear-engined coaches has established a niche for itself in Britain, especially in the small sector for double-deck coaches. The most common and, indeed, the most ostentatious is the N122 Skyliner double-decker — a 12m-long, 4m-high three-axle model with Mercedes V10, Gardner or Cummins engine. The 3.5m-high Mercedes V8-engined N116 Cityliner and N117 Spaceliner single-deckers have low driving positions and windscreens with raked top halves; the N117 has seats above the driver. Most conventional is the N216 Jetliner with Scania, DAF or Mercedes engines and a driving position only slightly lower than the passenger area. The 9.9m N212H midicoach is lower and has the Mercedes OM401LA engine.

After testing market demand in 1991 for two cheaper Mercedes V8-engined N316 Transliners built in Berlin, Neoplan changed tack and imported the Transliner on the Dennis Javelin chassis — a combination that offers a premium-looking body on a less expensive mid-engined chassis. An MAN 18.350 version followed in 1998.

ABOVE: *Neoplan: A Transliner-bodied Dennis Javelin operating with Buddens of Romsey on a contract for tour operator Insight.* **Dennis**

LEFT: *Neoplan: A tri-axle N116 Cityliner waiting for tourists at Stratford-upon-Avon. Double-deckers are very similar in appearance, apart from the obvious addition of a bottom deck.*

Noge

Built: Arbucies, Spain
Chassis: MAN 18.310, 14.220 and 24.400

Noge came on to the British market in 1997 in an exclusive deal with MAN. Its 3.5m-high Catalan 350 body, similar in concept to the highfloor Beulas body on the Iveco EuroRider, is fitted on the 12m 18.310 chassis. The 3.7m-high Catalan 370 is offered on the three-axle 24.400 and the 3.4m-high, 9.7m-long Catalan 340 is available on the 14.220.

LEFT: Noge: A 3.7m-high Catalan 370 body on one of the first MAN 24.400 six-wheel chassis imported to Britain.
Bus & Coach Buyer

Optare Solera

Built: Norena, Spain
Chassis: Mercedes-Benz O1120L

The 35-seat Solera, launched in 1997, is Optare's attempt to fill the same market niche as the Indcar Maxim, but with a rather more conservative design. Although badged as an Optare, the Solera — Spanish for highest quality — is built by Carrocerias Ferqui, a family-owned midicoach manufacturer.

RIGHT:

Optare Solera: The Spanish-built Solera offers a Mercedes midicoach that fits between the light truck-derived Vario and more substantial full-size coaches.

Plaxton Panorama Elite, Supreme, Viewmaster and Paramount

Built: Scarborough, North Yorkshire
Chassis: AEC Reliance; Bedford Y-Series, PJK, NJM; Ford R-Series; Leyland Leopard, Tiger, Royal Tiger; Bristol RE, LH; Volvo B58, B9M, B10M; DAF MB, SB; Seddon Pennine 7; Mercedes-Benz O303; Scania K92/93, K112/113; Neoplan N722; Dennis Dorchester, Javelin

Plaxton's Panorama Elite set a new trend for bow-sided coaches when it was launched in 1968. Models built before 1974 have their offside emergency exit directly behind the driver's cab; later examples have it just behind the rear axle. Dual-purpose models, called Elite Express, have two-piece doors and a wider entrance. On 11m and 12m versions, there is a short window immediately behind the entrance on the nearside.

The Supreme was introduced from 1974, with all-metal construction being phased in gradually on this model. Standard versions have taller side windows than the Elite, there is no beading above those windows and the windscreen and back window are more pointed on coaches built before 1978; they also have a taller grille to avoid fitting extra slats on vehicles like the LH and Ford which have front radiators. The high-floor Viewmaster, with taller windscreen and entrance/cab glazing, was added to the range in 1977.

From 1978, the earlier versions were replaced by the Supreme IV (with a more level windscreen) and an updated Viewmaster, both with redesigned grille and square headlamps. GT models launched a couple of years later had

BELOW: Plaxton Panorama Elite: One of the first 12m coaches to operate in Britain, this early Elite is on an AEC Reliance chassis. It was still operating with Chiltern Queens in Berkshire in 1994.

mesh rather than slatted grilles, but Plaxton also offered the new front panels to operators wishing to modernise older Supreme and Elite models, so be warned that all is not always what it might at first seem.

In 1981, the Supreme V replaced the IV. It has a flat, single-piece back window and larger tail lamps. It was accompanied by the Supreme VI — Plaxton's answer to the Duple Dominant III — with flat, shallow side windows for long distance work.

In 1982, the Ogle-designed Paramount was launched, retaining the shape of its predecessors, but with square-edged side windows. There were three models: the 3.2m-high 3200; 3.5m-high 3500; and the 4m-high 4000 — a double-decker on six-wheel Neoplan, Scania and DAF chassis and the 4000RS version with rear saloon on Volvo's six-wheel B10MT. Most 3200 and 3500 models have a short 'feature' window behind the first main side window which itself sweeps down towards the front. The windscreen was single-piece on the 3200 and horizontally divided on the 3500.

The 1985 MkII was available with optional bonded glazing and, in 1987, the range was restyled as the MkIII with bonded glazing only, and with the 'feature' window moved to immediately behind the cab/entrance. The grille was also restyled and horizontally divided windscreens became standard with the top raked back on the 3500. The Paramount range — still Britain's best-selling coach body — went out of production in 1991.

ABOVE: *Plaxton Supreme: Typical of a disappearing breed of once common coach, this Bedford PJK has the 29-seat version of the Supreme body.*

BELOW: *Plaxton Supreme VI: Shallow side windows distinguish the Supreme VI, here on a Leyland Tiger operated by Rochdale-based Ellen Smith, a long-established coach fleet now part of council-owned Rossendale Transport.*

LEFT: *Plaxton Paramount: An early Paramount 3200 with gasket-glazed windows on a Leyland Tiger chassis. New to NBC's London Country for Green Line routes, it was operating in 1991 with London Central, now a Go Ahead company but then part of London Buses.*

RIGHT: *Plaxton Paramount: A later Paramount 3500, with centre Continental door, on a Volvo B10M chassis. The coach alongside is a Paramount 3200 — note the height difference in the top part of the windscreen. Cambridge Coach Services is a Blazefield company.*

LEFT: *Plaxton Paramount: A Paramount 4000 double-decker on DAF SB3000 three-axle chassis.*

Plaxton Première, Prima and Excalibur

Built: Scarborough, North Yorkshire
Chassis: Volvo B10M, B7R, B12T; DAF SB3000; Dennis Javelin

The first totally new Plaxton coach range in 23 years was launched in the autumn of 1991. In place of the bow sides of the previous models, the Première and Excalibur have flat sides and back. The 3.2m high Première and 3.5m-high Première 350 have a very upright front with a single-piece windscreen on the lower model and a horizontally divided one on the 350. The top-of-the-range Excalibur has a raked front with a thicker pillar behind the entrance/cab, rather like the Marcopolo Explorer and Wright Contour. An export model, the 3.7m Prestige, was developed on left-hand-drive two-axle B12s, primarily for an unsuccessful move into the French market. The Prestige name has since been used for Plaxton's 12m lowfloor bus body. For Stagecoach, a dual-purpose Première — known initially as the Interurban — was developed and some of these have opening side windows. With the launch of Volvo's B7R in 1997, the Interurban specification was refined and renamed the Prima. Whatever the model name, most of the range has been built as 12m coaches, but Stagecoach has a batch of 10 Interurban 18m articulated B10Ms; it also has 11m Javelins (with opening side windows) while Ashford Luxury, in Middlesex, got the first 9.7m Première — also on a Javelin — in 1994.

ABOVE RIGHT:
Plaxton Première: The first 9.7m version of the 3.2m-high Première was built in 1994 on a Dennis Javelin for Ashford Luxury.

RIGHT: *Plaxton Première: The Première 350, seen here on a Volvo B10M chassis, has additional glazing above the entrance door.*
Plaxton

When the new range was launched a few Scanias were bodied, but initial production was confined to Volvo and Dennis, with DAF offering the Première 350 from 1996 and the Interurban/ Prima from 1997.

ABOVE: *Plaxton Excalibur: The curved front of the Excalibur transforms the appearance of the otherwise standard Plaxton body. This is on a relatively rare six-wheel Volvo B12T.* ***Plaxton***

Reeve Burgess Harrier

Built: Pilsley, Derbyshire
Chassis: Leyland Swift

Reeve Burgess introduced the Harrier body on the Leyland Swift in 1988. It has square-edged gasket windows and a large single-piece windscreen. The recessed area around the wiper mechanism creates the illusion of a deeper central section to the windscreen. There also are a few bus versions.

BELOW: *Reeve Burgess: The Harrier body, on Leyland Swift chassis, was usually built as a coach, but the bus version seen here is externally identical save for the folding doors in place of the standard one-piece coach door.*

Setra

Built: Ulm, Germany; Ligny-en-Barrois, France; Samano, Spain 1976 to date

Engines: Mercedes OM422 and 442 V8, OM421 V6; Cummins L10; MAN D2866

Transmission: ZF synchromesh or automatic

The Setra integral coach (the name comes from German 'selbst tragend' meaning 'self supporting') has been sold continuously in Britain since 1981 and is built by Evobus, a company formed in 1995 by Mercedes to take over the bus and coach manufacturing operations of Kassböhrer which built the Setra before then. Evobus has since merged the sales and marketing organisations for Setra and Mercedes buses and coaches sold in the UK.

The 3.4m-high V6-engined S210HD (8.9m- and 12m-long) and S215HD (12m with V8 engine or Spanish-built, MAN-powered Tornado) coaches have bowed sides, bonded glazing and curvaceous front and rear windscreens.

The S228DT Imperial six-wheel double-decker bears a strong family resemblance. The French-built S215HR Rational is a cheaper 3.3m-high V8-engined single-decker with front drum brakes instead of discs and either gasket or bonded glazing.

Setra launched a new S300 Series in mainland Europe in 1991, but has still to sell it in Britain. In 1995, it made a step in that direction by replacing the S200 with the S250 which combines the front end and 'rabbit ears' mirrors of the new model with the main body of the S200; there is a choice of OM442 or MAN engine.

BELOW: *Setra: An S215 operated by Seamarks of Luton. Later models have a less elaborate grille.*

TOP RIGHT: *Setra: A Setra S250 at Stansted Airport, Eurolines is the European express coach network, the British and Dutch parts of which are owned by National Express.*

Smit Euroliner and Orion

Built: Joure, Netherlands
Chassis: DAF MB, SB

Smit — owned by DAF Bus since 1996 — supplied a few coach bodies on DAF mid- and rear-engined chassis between 1982 and 1985. First model into Britain was the Euroliner, with an upright front, divided windscreen and a vague hint of Van Hool styling. It has a flat rear window. It was followed by the Orion, with a more raked front.

BELOW: *Smit: A Smit Euroliner on a rear-engined DAF SB chassis operated by Kettlewell's of Retford. To the left is the back of a Leyland National Mk1 (see single-deck bus section).*

TAZ Dubrava

Built: Zagreb, Croatia
Engine: Mercedes OM422 V8
Transmission: ZF synchromesh

More than 60 Dubravas were imported between 1988 and 1990, filling the gap in the market left when Bova replaced the Europa with the Futura. Unlike the Charisma, this Yugoslavian coach bears no outward resemblance to the Mercedes O.303, but it does have a Mercedes engine. There are two versions: the 3.2m-high 3200 and the 3.5m 3500.

LEFT: A Dubrava 3200 operated by Hi-Lite Travel, a West Midlands operator that bought several of these coaches and a supply of replacement parts to go with them.

UVG UniStar and S320

Built: Waterlooville, Hampshire
Chassis: Dennis Javelin

When it took over Wadham Stringer (see single-deck bus section), UVG inherited a substantial order book for Ministry of Defence coaches on Dennis Javelin chassis. The body style, known initially as the Vanguard III, was updated for civilian customers and christened the UniStar, but still looked more like a bus than a coach. So it was developed in 1997 into the S320, a budget-priced high-capacity coach aimed at the school transport and private hire markets. Standard versions came with 57 fixed seats, but up to 69 could be fitted in on a three-and-two basis (three seats on one side of the aisle and two on the other). The S320 has a hint of Plaxton Première in its very upright front. The cost of developing the S320 was one of the factors that led to receivers being called into UVG's Waterlooville bus division later in 1997 and the subsequent sale of the company to Salvador Caetano UK.

BELOW: UVG: A UVG UniStar body on an 8.5m Dennis Javelin. This 31-seater was supplied in 1997 to a Hampshire coach operator. Dennis

136

ABOVE: *UVG: A 69-seat S320-bodied Javelin enjoys a prominent position at Coach & Bus '97, raised on column lifts for a workshop.*

Van Hool T8 and T9

Built: Lier, Belgium
Chassis: Leyland Tiger, Royal Tiger; DAF MB, SB; Volvo B9M, B10M, B12T; Scania K-Series, N112, N113; Dennis Lancet; integrals

Van Hool launched its T8 range of bodies and integrals in 1980, keeping the basic design for the next 17 years, save for some relatively cosmetic changes over that period. Hallmarks of the design are its gently curved front and a shallow barrel-shaped back window. The most common T8 in Britain is the 3.4m- and 3.6m-high Alizée body on Volvo, DAF and Scania chassis. Others in the range are: T812 10m integral with MAN D2866 vertical rear engine; T815 3.4m-high Alicron and 3.6m Acron integrals with D2866,

Cummins L10 or DAF 11.6-litre engine; T818 3.9m Astron with mid-underfloor MAN engine and rear saloon; 4m Astral on three-axle B10MT also with rear

BELOW: *Van Hool: A contrast in windscreen designs on two Alizée T8s in the Ellen Smith fleet. The Tiger on the right has a low driving position and horizontally divided windscreen, while the Volvo B10M on the left has a higher cockpit with vertically divided screen.*

saloon; T824 4m-high Astromega double-decker with Mercedes-Benz OM422 V8 engine; and 4m Astrobel double-deck body on three-axle DAF SB3000, Scania K112/K113 and Volvo B12T chassis. A few Alizée bus bodies have been built on Volvo B10M and Scania N113 chassis.

In 1997, Van Hool introduced its new T9 range which uses the same model names, even though the styling is very different with swept-down front side windows and a tall back window. Initially, only the T9 Alizée was being sold in Britain, but an Astrobel double-decker has also been developed.

BELOW: *Van Hool: A T8 Astrobel double-decker, on Volvo B12T, stands ahead of an Alizée-bodied B10M in Sheffield Interchange. The double-decker was operating with National Express contractor Trathens of Plymouth, part of the Scottish-based Park's Motor Group.*

RIGHT: *Van Hool: A T9 Alizée-bodied Scania L94 for The Kings Ferry.*

Van Hool EOS

Built: Bree, Belgium
Engines: MAN D2866, Mercedes-Benz OM441LA V6
Transmission: ZF synchromesh

After taking over LAG and renaming the business the EOS Coach Manufacturing Company, Van Hool redesigned and expanded the rear-engined range, giving it a more conventional front. Smallest model is the Mercedes-engined EOS 80, a 9.5m-long, 3.4m-high midi with up to 41 seats; next up is the EOS 90, a 3.45m-high 12m coach; and the range in Britain is topped by the 3.7m-high, three-axle EOS 230. The 90 and 230 have the MAN engine; the 80 and 90 have a single-piece windscreen, the 230 a two-piece horizontally divided windscreen.

BELOW: *Van Hool EOS: A three-axle EOS 230 operated by Hallmark Cars on prestigious football team contracts. Despite its full 12m length, this vehicle only has 28 seats as it is packed with a host of other comforts including a large kitchen area at the back.* **Arriva Bus & Coach**

Volvo C10M

Built: Biel, Switzerland 1984-6
Engine: Volvo THD100
Transmission: ZF synchromesh or automatic

Ten of Volvo's short-lived, high specification 3.4m-high integral C10M coaches were imported into Britain. The Swedish underframe was fitted in a body built under licence by Swiss urban bus builder Ramseier & Jenzer. The design maximised luggage space by fitting its mid-engine just ahead of the rear axle and also by giving it a long wheelbase with a short front overhang.

LEFT: *Volvo C10M: Two C10Ms in the Seamarks fleet show off the offside and nearside front of these unusual coaches. They have offside cab doors and a rear Continental door. Note also the péage window in the nearside door.*

Willowbrook Crusader

Built: Loughborough, Leicestershire
Chassis: Leyland Leopard, Tiger; AEC
Reliance; Bedford Y-Series; Ward
Dalesman

When Willowbrook rose from
the ashes in 1985, it developed
the Crusader, with gasket
glazing and flat side windows,
for new Bedford and Tiger
chassis. Most of the handful
built went, instead, on
reconditioned Leopards and a
Reliance. In 1991, one of the
last went on the final one of the
very few Yorkshire-built Ward
Dalesman mid-engined chassis.

BELOW: *Willowbrook Crusader:
Spalding in Lincolnshire is the location of
this view of a rare Crusader body, with a
Plaxton Supreme parked behind.*

Wright Contour

Built: Ballymena, Co Antrim
Chassis: Bedford YNT, Venturer,
Leyland Tiger, ACE Puma, Ford T152

Before becoming a major player in the
bus market, Wright's worked closely
with General Motors' styling people to
develop the 1982 Contour, an
aluminium-framed body offered at first
only on the Bedford YNT. The raked

front and deep curved windscreen were
nearly 10 years ahead of the Plaxton
Excalibur. On some, the rear wheels are
boxed in. Most Contours are 11m or
12m long, but 8m versions were built
on the ACE Puma (out of the same
stable as the Cougar mentioned under
Wadham Stringer and Willowbrook in
the single-deck bus section) and Ford's
short R-Series, the T152.

LEFT: *Wright
Contour: The Wright
coach anticipated the
design trends of the
1990s, but sold in
only small numbers.
This one was outside
the Waldorf, one of
London's most famous
hotels, in May 1994.*

Part 4. MINIBUSES

Many mini and midibuses are developed from mass-produced vans and light trucks, although there also are purpose-built vehicles. Space precludes inclusion of the first generation of minibuses converted from Ford Transit and Freight Rover Sherpa vans, as these have now largely disappeared from major fleets. This section provides identification detail on the vans and light trucks from which the main surviving types are based as well as providing more detail of the coachbuilt bodies and complete vehicles at the larger end of the mini/midi scale. Most of the minibus types are used very widely around the country.

Chassis and Base Vans

Iveco DailyBus

Built: Brescia and Suzzara,
Italy 1978 to date
Engine: Iveco diesel
Transmission: Synchromesh
or automatic
Bodywork: Carlyle, Dormobile,
Robin Hood, LHE, Phoenix, Reeve
Burgess, Mellor, Carlyle, CarChair,
Alexander, Marshall.

The DailyBus is based on the 4.2-tonne 40.8, 5-tonne 49.10, 5.2-tonne 49.12 and 6-tonne 59.12 light truck chassis/bonnet cowls for bodies with up to 28 seats. Smaller versions of the Daily are sold as van conversion minibuses. Pre-1989 models have flat grilles and round headlamps; later models have a more pointed bonnet with a smaller grille between square headlamps. Some bodybuilders disguise the bonnet with their own design.

BELOW: *Iveco DailyBus: A Carlyle-bodied 49.12 in the Streamline livery used by FirstGroup for some local services in Bath. Streamline was an independent company taken over by FirstGroup's Bristol Omnibus Company.*

Mercedes-Benz L608D, T2 and Vario

Built: Düsseldorf, Germany 1967 to date
Engine: Mercedes diesel
Transmission: Mercedes or ZF synchromesh or Mercedes or Allison automatic
Bodywork: Carlyle, Dormobile, Robin Hood, LHE, Phoenix, Plaxton/Reeve Burgess, Mellor, Carlyle, Alexander, Marshall, PMT, Europa, Autobus Classique, Crystals, Wadham Stringer, UVG, Optare, Wright.

National Bus Company subsidiaries were keen late purchasers of the L608D van conversion which Mercedes supplied straight from its production line with a bus back. As a 20-seater, it represented the first step ahead of the 16-seat Transit and has also proved to be very durable. It is identifiable by a single-piece windscreen with quarterlights.

The successor T2 range, launched in 1986, is most common as a chassis/cowl with coachbuilt bodywork, but there also are van conversions. Buses are based on the 5.6-tonne 609, 6.6-tonne 709 and 711, and 7.2-tonne 811 and 814.

In a further change, the T2 evolved into the Vario, with Euro 2 engines, in 1996/7. This has a revised grille style and the bus models sold are the O810D and O814D with 102 and 136hp engines respectively and a choice of ZF synchromesh or Allison automatic transmission.

BELOW: Mercedes-Benz L608D: This Reeve Burgess-converted 608 began life with Lincolnshire Road Car when it was a National Bus Company fleet. Road Car was bought by Yorkshire Traction, owner of former Scottish Bus Group fleet Strathtay, to which the bus was subsequently transferred. It was photographed in Dundee.

Renault (Dodge) S56, S75

Built: Dunstable, Bedfordshire 1979-93
Engine: Perkins diesel
Transmission: Synchromesh, Chrysler or Allison automatic
Bodywork: Alexander, East Lancs, Northern Counties, Reeve Burgess

The Renault light truck began life as the Dodge 50 and many of the earlier bus versions were badged as such, often also with Renault diamond logos. Like the Iveco and Mercedes T2, they were supplied as chassis/cowls, although some bodybuilders have fitted their own bonnet designs. The S56 is a 6-tonne 25-seater; the S75 a 33-seat 7.5-tonner designed for bus operation. London Buses bought a comparatively large fleet of S75s with Wright and Reeve Burgess bodies; the former have been dispersed among some FirstGroup fleets, the latter were bought by Yorkshire Traction and its subsidiaries Road Car and Strathtay.

BELOW: *Renault/Dodge S56: A Travel Dundee S56 with an example of the original style of Alexander AM body with lower window line.*

Talbot/TBP/Crystals Pullman/ Freeway II

Built: Coventry; Birmingham; Doncaster 1986 to date
Engine: Sofim diesel.
Transmission: Synchromesh.
Bodywork: TBP, Crystals

The six-wheel Pullman was developed in Britain from the Italian-built Express van, a joint venture between the Fiat and Peugeot groups. Its small wheels and front-wheel-drive gave it a low floor only 20in from the ground, making it particularly useful for dial-a-rides and other services aimed at the needs of disabled people. The Pullman name is

143

from an old Humber limousine built by Rootes whose business is now owned by Peugeot. In 1990, production rights were sold to TBP which continued to manufacture and market the vehicle as a Talbot until the Express was replaced by the Peugeot Boxer — another joint venture product with Fiat. TBP invested £1.25 million in developing the Freeway II (the previous Freeway was a welfare version of the Pullman) which is unmistakable in having a low front section and a raised rear section. Few were bought by anyone, least of all for bus work, but Pathfinder of Newark was an enthusiastic purchaser before it was taken over by Nottingham City Transport. TBP went into receivership in 1996 and the Freeway II design rights were bought by Crystals which planned to build it in South Yorkshire.

BELOW: *Talbot Pullman: A six-wheel lowfloor Pullman in local bus service in Helensburgh, Dunbartonshire.*

BELOW: *TBP Freeway II: The raised roof at the rear of the Freeway II makes it quite unlike any other minibus produced in recent years.* **Bus & Coach Buyer**

Alexander AM Sprint, ALX100

Built: Falkirk, Stirlingshire; Mallusk, Co Antrim 1985 to date

Chassis: Mercedes 709, 811, 814, Vario; Renault S56, S75; Iveco DailyBus.

When big bus orders dried up in the mid-1980s, Alexander converted some Mercedes L608D vans into minibuses, then developed its own coachbuilt aluminium-framed body, the AM-type, for Renault S56 chassis/cowls. The first examples have low-set side windows and a heavy-looking roof, but the design evolved quickly as it became available on Mercedes T2 chassis/cowls and gained high-set windows, taller windscreens and a larger destination box. An Iveco was bodied for evaluation by Stagecoach, which has large fleets on Mercedes 709D chassis. When Alexander adopted model names from 1993, the AM became the AM Sprint. It evolved again in 1997 into the ALX100, the least radically different of the new body family; it has flat sides, square-edged gasket glazing and round tail lamps.

LEFT: Alexander AM Sprint: Compare this with the Renault/Dodge on page 143. This shows the later version of AM Sprint, with higher window line, on a Mercedes 709D operated by Great Yarmouth independent Flying Banana which has since been taken over by First Eastern Counties. This body was also offered with square-edged windows.

*LEFT: Alexander ALX100: A Midland Red (now Arriva Midlands North) Mercedes Vario O814 with the latest style of Alexander minibus body. **Alexander***

145

Autobus

Built: Rotherham, South Yorkshire
1991 to date
Chassis: Mercedes 811, 814, Vario

An Optare subsidiary since 1996, Autobus was formed in 1991 by some former managers of Doncaster-based Europa, which had bodied Mercedes and Renault minibuses for Yorkshire Traction, among others, and which had just collapsed. Until Optare took over, it was called Autobus Classique and it came to specialise more in building small luxury coaches, culminating in the Nouvelle which was developed in its last months of independence. Under Optare ownership, the Nouvelle 2 with restyled windscreen, grille and headlamp areas appeared in 1997 and the company moved to a larger factory in Rotherham in 1998. The Nouvelle 2 sells in part of the market Optare supplied earlier with its StarRider coach.

BELOW: *Autobus Nouvelle 2: The latest style of Nouvelle body, developed following the Optare takeover, on a Mercedes Vario chassis. Earlier versions have provision for a destination box or operator's illuminated name board above a shallower windscreen.* ***Optare***

Marshall (and Carlyle)

Built: Edgbaston, Birmingham 1989-91; Cambridge 1992 to date
Chassis: Mercedes-Benz 811D, 814D, Vario; Iveco DailyBus

Carlyle moved from van conversions to coachbuilt minibuses with a flat-sided body with a destination box standing proud of the roof dome. Shortly before the business collapsed, it built a prototype body for the DailyBus 59.12 with a Cromweld structure and this was put into production at Cambridge after Marshall bought the business. It was restyled with a peaked roof dome in 1997 and named the Master.

ABOVE: *Marshall: The original Carlyle body design was kept in production by Marshall. This is on a Mercedes 811D operating with Streamline of Bath before it was bought by FirstGroup.*

ABOVE: *Marshall: The Marshall Master body on a Mercedes Vario O 814 in First Thamesway livery. The main design change is to the roof dome and destination box.*

Northern Counties

Built: Wigan, Greater Manchester
1986-92

Chassis: Renault S56

Northern Counties was one of the first traditional bus builders to diversify into minibuses, starting with a utilitarian van-like body married to the standard S56 bonnet and windscreen. It replaced this with a design with a taller, arched windscreen, before producing a third and final version in 1988, with a coachbuilt bonnet and grille. Although given the Pageant model name in 1992, Northern Counties by then was concentrating on larger vehicles.

ABOVE: *Northern Counties: The final version of the Northern Counties body, on a Nottingham City Transport Renault S56, showing the disguising effect of the coachbuilt front end.*

Omni

Built: Shildon, Co Durham 1988
to date

Engines: Land Rover, Perkins,
Mazda or Iveco diesel

Transmission: ZF synchromesh or automatic, Quaife synchromesh.

The integral lowfloor Omni, with front-wheel-drive, air suspension and four or six wheels, is an Austrian design manufactured in Britain. It was too late into the market to sell well into major bus fleets, but had more success in the welfare market where it offered real benefits for carrying people in wheelchairs. It suffered, nonetheless, from a reputation for poor reliability and both City Vehicle Engineering — the company formed to build it — and Omni Coach which succeeded it in 1991 went into receivership. It was rescued again in 1997 by another company, FTL Omni, which announced plans for a major redesign likely to see the light of day during 1998. FTL was concentrating on building them with Iveco engines and gearboxes by Quaife, a Kent racing car engineering company which had already made replacement 'boxes for older Omnis. In 1998, three battery electric six-wheel Omnis were delivered to Strathclyde PTE which had plans to operate them in Glasgow city centre; Whippet Coaches operates six-wheel diesels on rural routes into Cambridge

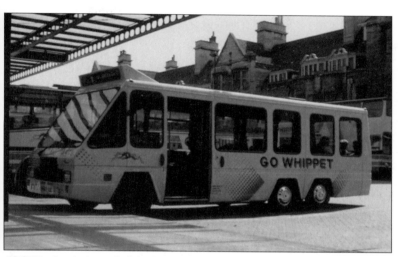

ABOVE: *Omni: A six-wheel Omni operating with Whippet Coaches in Cambridge on a lowfloor service part-funded by the Rural Development Commission.*

Optare CityPacer, StarRider

Built: Leeds 1986-93
Chassis: Volkswagen LT55, Mercedes-Benz 811D, 814D

In 1986, the CityPacer set the trend for minibuses with raked fronts and did more than many to lead the move away from the first generation of 'bread vans'. It was styled by Leeds art students and based on a 5.5-tonne Volkswagen van not normally sold in the UK. The chassis, with a choice of synchromesh or Allison automatic gearbox, was rebuilt with a higher driving position moved behind, rather than over the front axle, and with outriggers added to take bodywork with seats arranged four abreast. Most were built as buses, but there was an Inter-CityPacer coach.

Although eye catching, the CityPacer was soon left behind by the trend towards larger minibuses and, in 1987, the StarRider was launched to offer a similarly packaged 33-seat product on the Mercedes 811D chassis and later on the more powerful 814D. The windscreen is shallower than on the CityPacer, and the body has four full bays rather than three-and-a-half, but the original Mercedes bonnet assembly is discarded in favour of Optare's coachbuilt front. A coach version remained in low volume production for longer than the bus. In 1990, the cheaper StarRider SRe — with Mercedes bonnet and windscreen — was launched, but very few were built.

ABOVE: *Optare CityPacer: A Reading Buses CityPacer shows off the striking windscreen design 10 years after it first took to the streets.*

ABOVE: *Optare StarRider: The shallower windscreen and, where fitted as on this First Badgerline example in Bath, the Mercedes badge are key identification features on the StarRider.*

Optare MetroRider (and MCW Metrorider)

Built: Birmingham 1986-9;
Leeds 1989 to date.
Engines: Cummins 6B, Perkins Phaser
Transmission: Allison or Chrysler
automatic, ZF synchromesh.

The steel-framed integral Metrorider began life as an MCW product, the first urban midibus designed as such from the outset. Styling clearly was influenced by the Optare CityPacer, but with taller windows and a shallower roof. MCW sold more than 1,000 in 7m (up to 25 seats) and 8.4m (up to 33 seats) lengths, 2.2m and 2.4m widths, a choice of two engines and three gearboxes and finished as a bus or coach. Customers included some large fleets, but MCW lost money developing and selling it, so ironically the volume

of sales contributed to the company's decision to close in 1989.

Optare turned itself into a complete vehicle builder when it bought the design. It re-spelt its name as MetroRider, beefed up the mechanical specification (standardising on the Cummins/Allison driveline) and simplified the body — notably by replacing MCW's stretched steel side panels with short aluminium ones, fitting glassfibre skirts from the StarRider, going for gasket glazing instead of bonded glass, and straight side windows instead of the MCW design that swept up slightly towards the back. While MCW fitted divided windscreens on buses and single-piece screens on the handful of coaches built, Optare went for single-piece windscreens on most narrow versions. A 7.7m-long intermediate length MetroRider was added in 1993 when

ABOVE: *MCW Metrorider: A short Birmingham-built Metrorider with MCW badge above the registration number plate and the slightly upward-tapering rearmost side window.*

the range was modified to incorporate Euro 1 engines, a larger destination display and wider entrance. In 1995, when combined MCW and Optare production of the model passed 2,000, a slightly lower floor was fitted. Less conventional versions are compressed natural gas (CNG) fuelled versions with Stagecoach Cambus in Cambridge and Reading Buses in Newbury (the Reading vehicles have modified Rover V8 petrol engines) and battery electrics run for a time in Oxford. Major users of MetroRiders include several London operators, Reading Buses, Wilts & Dorset, Cardiff, Newport, Trent, SMT/Lowland, Ipswich, Blackpool, Nottingham, Arriva North East, Arriva Yorkshire, Arriva Scotland West and Go Ahead North East.

ABOVE: *Optare MetroRider: A Leeds-built MetroRider with the later style of longer body with wider door and restyled destination box.* **Optare**

Optare Solo

Built: Leeds 1997 to date
Engines: Mercedes-Benz OM904LA
Transmission: Allison automatic

In the longer term, Optare expects that the Solo — named because its 250mm step height is 'so low' — will replace the MetroRider. It has a similar integral steel structure to both the MetroRider and the Excel and, when launched, was the most practical lowfloor mini/midibus yet produced. It looks a little like a cross between the MetroRider and the CityPacer, with a deep, barrel-shaped windscreen and bonded glazing. The lowfloor layout is achieved by fitting a four-cylinder Mercedes engine in the back. There is no rear window, largely because the engine occupies most of the space needed to make one practical. It is a full 2.5m wide and is offered in two lengths, 8.5m and 9.2m — seating up to 33 or 37 respectively. Early Solo customers include Wilts & Dorset (for routes in Poole, Bournemouth and Salisbury), Reading Buses and Travel West Midlands (for operation in the West Midlands and by its associate fleets in London and Dundee).

ABOVE: *Optare Solo: The first of 85 Solos for Wilts & Dorset, a 30-seat 8.5m model. Note the vast windscreen in relation to the size of the bus.* **Optare**

Plaxton (and Reeve Burgess) Beaver, Cheetah

Built: Pilsley, Derbyshire; Scarborough, North Yorkshire; Anston, South Yorkshire.
Chassis: Mercedes-Benz T2, Vario; Renault S56, S75; Iveco DailyBus.

The steel-framed, square-windowed Beaver is the best-selling minibus body in Britain. It was launched in 1987, replacing an earlier Reeve Burgess design with round-edged windows. When the Pilsley works closed in 1991, production was transferred to the then-underutilised Plaxton coach plant in Scarborough and the model was

BELOW: *Plaxton Beaver: An example of the earlier style of Beaver, on a Mercedes 811D of First Cymru, the trading name of South Wales Transport.* **Plaxton**

rebranded soon after as a Plaxton. By then, it was only being built on Mercedes chassis. Coach sales picked up sufficiently for Plaxton to transfer Beaver bus production to part of its Anston site in 1995.

The Beaver has been built in various lengths and widths, as a bus and as a coach. By 1991, the original roof-height destination box was replaced by a taller unit standing proud of the roof dome. In 1997, the Ogle-styled Beaver 2 bus was launched on the new Vario and the Scarborough-built Cheetah, with coachbuilt front, replaced the Beaver coach.

LEFT: *Plaxton Beaver 2: The restyling of the Beaver, for the Mercedes Vario chassis, significantly alters its appearance, giving it curved rather than squared-off roof edges.* **Plaxton**

BELOW: *Plaxton Cheetah: The Vario-based Cheetah gives Plaxton's small minibus the appearance of a proper small coach to compete against vehicles like the Autobus Nouvelle.*

PMT Ami

Built: Stoke-on-Trent, Staffordshire.
Chassis: Mercedes-Benz 811D.

PMT Engineering followed the raked-front trend in 1989 with the Ami which sold mostly to its own bus fleet. It has shallow side windows, an integrated destination box and windscreen and has a shallow grille between the headlamps.

BELOW: PMT Ami: A First PMT-owned Ami, on Mercedes 811D chassis, at work in Hanley, in the heart of the Staffordshire Potteries.

Robin Hood

Built: Eastleigh, Hampshire

Chassis: (RH2000) Mercedes-Benz 814D, Vario; Iveco 59.12; Cannon Softline

Robin Hood was one of the major suppliers of minibuses to the National Bus Company in the mid-1980s, first with van conversions, later with coachbuilt bodies on the Iveco Daily. It went on to develop a larger version for the increasingly popular Mercedes T2 range, but from 1989 the company went through a period of trauma with successor companies Phoenix, LHE and CarChair all eventually hitting trouble. The business was revived only to go into receivership again in 1998. In 1997, it began production of the RH2000, a midicoach with a heavily raked, curved front; on some, the complete front end (including windscreen) lifts up for maintenance. The Cannon Softline is a new Northern Ireland-built chassis with front-mounted Cummins 6BT engine.

155

ABOVE: *Robin Hood: A late example of Robin Hood's bus body on a Solent Blue Line Mercedes in Southampton.*

RIGHT:
Robin Hood: An RH2000 body, on a Mercedes Vario, with luxury coach operator Hallmark Cars.

Toyota Optimo

Built: Oporto, Portugal 1985 to date
Engine: Toyota diesel
Transmission: Toyota synchromesh.

Toyota's Coaster is one of the world's best-selling buses. For the British market, it is assembled and bodied in Portugal by Caetano, which is 27% owned by Toyota, and sold as the Optimo coach. Models sold until 1990 have an upright profile. The successor Optimo II, III and IV have a rounded profile and raked windscreen; the III and IV have an offside cab door. A 2.3m-wide version was launched in 1997, with up to 26 seats instead of the maximum of 21 on the 2.12m-wide version sold until then. All are 7.5m long. In 1985, Caetano also imported the Viana, similar in style to the original Optimo, but based on the Iveco 79.14 truck and with its front axle set back to accommodate a narrow entrance on the front overhang.

ABOVE: *Caetano Viana: The Iveco-based Viana and early Toyota Optimos all had this fairly square, upright body style. The Viana's entrance is ahead of the front axle.*

ABOVE: *Toyota Optimo: An Optimo III, showing the later style of body with curved lines and cab door. This one has air conditioning, hence the grille behind the front wheel.*

UVG/Wadham Stringer/WS Coachbuilders

Built: Waterlooville, Hampshire
Chassis: Mercedes-Benz T2, Vario; Iveco DailyBus 59.12

Wadham Stringer had as small a share of the minibus market as it did in the larger single-deck and coach sectors. Its original Wessex design, with round-edged windows, found few buyers, but a batch built for Bournemouth Yellow Buses was sold on to Brighton & Hove and was still in that fleet in 1998. The Wessex II, launched in 1993 when the company was renamed WS — and fitted with shorter, square-edged windows — sold better if mainly to small operators. This model was renamed CityStar in 1995 when the company name changed to UVG. Production transferred to UVG's Welsh plant before the Waterlooville operation was placed in receivership.

LEFT: WS Wessex II: Short, square-edged windows help identify the later style of Wessex, seen here in Reading with Surrey-based Tillingbourne Bus.

Wright NimBus

Built: Ballymena, Co Antrim
Chassis: Mercedes-Benz T2; Renault S75.

Wright's NimBus uses the same Alusuisse construction system as the larger bodies in its range — and the same thick rubber window gaskets. Operators include First Leicester and First BeeLine, Southern National, Stagecoach Midland Red and Red & White. British Airways crew buses at Heathrow and Gatwick airports are among the last NimBuses built before Wright's concentrated on larger vehicles.

RIGHT: Wright NimBus: A Mercedes 811D in a route-branded all-white livery for Trent. Wright

158

ABOVE: *Optare Solo: One of the first examples of the Optare Solo is seen in service with Wilts & Dorset in Bournemouth.* **Philip Lamb**